The Anxiety Conquering Workbook for Teens

Fun and Simple DBT-Based Exercises to Master Stress, Build Resilience, and Manage Your Emotions

Blake Cameron

Table Of Contents

Medical Disclaimer

This book's content is solely for informational purposes and should not be used to diagnose, treat, cure, or prevent any physical or mental medical conditions.

Introduction

Walking through the two large doors, Alex felt the weight of the entire school's judgmental eyes on him as he made his way down the hall toward his locker. He couldn't help but think that if he had done better during the championships, he wouldn't feel like such a failure.

Tammy fidgeted with her clothes while standing across from Alex. She couldn't help but notice how every girl that walked past her was thin and beautiful. Tammy wished she could look like them, but she couldn't afford the platinum blond hair or cool colors that so many of her classmates had. She felt like a sore thumb among them, as if a beacon hung over her head and pointed out how she wasn't like them.

James kept his head low as he walked down the hallway, worried that his 'C' grade was written all over his face. Despite his efforts, everything seemed to be falling apart. He had even asked Mr. Thomas for extra credit, but the teacher had dismissed his concerns, insisting that a 'C' wasn't the end of the world. However, for James, it was the one thing preventing him from getting into his dad's alma mater.

Sam sat with her head in a book, partly hidden by the staircase. She didn't want anyone to know that being around so many people made her sweaty and nervous. She longed to have friends and easily converse with others without freezing up, blurting out things, or feeling like she was about to faint. Hiding inside the worlds of her books helped her cope.

A group of friends laughed on the stairs, but Marcus felt pressure to conform and not be left out. He felt guilty for not spending time with his family because his friends preferred to spray paint the walls by the dumpsters of the local supermarket. Marcus feared getting caught and facing his parents' disappointment.

Abby always rushed through the halls to her class, never speaking to anyone. She got into fights with random people and was often absent. Rumors circulated that she was doing drugs, but the truth was that her parents were struggling with money, and she had taken on a part-time job with hectic hours. Between school, work, and preparing for college, she wasn't sleeping, and the more sleep she lost, the quicker she was to anger.

They were all in the same school, but each of them felt alone in the struggles of being a teenager, dealing with rollercoaster emotions, and feeling overwhelming anxiety every day.

Everyone experiences anxiety and moments of deep negative emotions. It's common to feel alone, out of control, or overwhelmed by emotions. Anxiety is not limited to teenagers, as adults also struggle with it. Therefore, it's crucial to learn the skills to conquer anxiety from an early age, so as to thrive in the situations that cause it in the long-term.

Life's Messy and That's Okay

There comes a time in our lives when we know—in the deepest parts of ourselves—we can't wing it anymore; a point where we can't wait and hope for things to sort themselves out or get better because we've done that already, and things didn't work themselves out, or they even became worse.

Life is messy and confusing. Sometimes it can feel like being thrown about in a tornado. But that's also life; it has ups and downs. Life has moments where you keep a cool head when things get hard, but then there are moments when you're not as cool-headed and start to bend under that pressure. And that's all okay. It's simply part of life.

Life changes—it never stays the same. Since birth, we're all constantly learning new things, coming to understand life, and learning about ourselves. We start by learning to crawl, then take shaky steps until we can walk, and once we can, we begin to run. This process also doesn't happen overnight; it takes time, but as we grow confident in what we can do, we become fearless and feel inspired and encouraged to try more new things. While not exactly the same as learning to conquer your anxieties, you'll still have to take the process slow, begin with small steps, and build your confidence in the skills you learn before you can begin to slay these anxieties once and for all.

But, you already know life is messy. You're already experiencing the changes your body and mind undergo as you progress through puberty, and as you learn to express your emotions and discover who you are. Sometimes, we need help in moving through these stages of life, as well as guidance to help us understand our feelings and thoughts. After all, you picked up this book because you want to understand what you are experiencing, learn to deal with it constructively and develop the necessary skills to help you thrive in life rather than just trying to survive from one moment to the next.

Reaping the Benefits

The skills and knowledge you'll gain from working through this book will help you navigate your teenage years and provide the insights you need to conquer any challenges and anxieties you may face later in life.

We have designed this workbook to help you gain the benefits of Dialectical Behavioral Therapy (DBT) in the following ways:

- by providing you with shortcuts into The Four Modules of DBT:

    - Core Mindfulness

    - Distress Tolerance

    - Emotion Regulation

    - Interpersonal Effectiveness

- by helping you find and practice your Wise Mind and learn how using your Wise Mind can benefit you in the long run.

- by teaching you how to self-soothe to manage the moments when you feel distressed.

- by providing you with Radical Acceptance statements that you can take anywhere with you.

- by providing you with Assertiveness Scripts that you can take anywhere with you and use when you feel overwhelmed.

- by learning the importance of why you need to set boundaries and how to set these boundaries.

The information gathered and laid out in this book is the accumulation of over 50 years of research and knowledge. Each method, module, and exercise were tried and tested until specific skills, activities, and techniques were found. DBT has helped millions upon millions of people: Selena Gomez, Lady Gaga, Brandon Marshall, Pete Davidson, Demi Lovato, and Alexandria Ocasio-Cortez are among the many people who have openly talked about using DBT skills in their daily lives. While other celebrities don't openly talk about DBT, many of them make use of the skills the therapy provides them with…as you'll come to see yourself soon.

The goal of this book is to help anyone who is struggling with regulating their emotions, managing their anxiety, and finding it difficult to express themselves, as well as those who are going through the stages of personal growth and self-discovery, and who think negatively about themselves, their life, or their future. By the time you've finished this book, you'll have the skills you need to regulate your emotions, manage your anxieties, express yourself safely and without fear, have a positive outlook on life and your future, and find an adaptive way to discover who you are and be confident in what you need, want, and expect from life and those around you.

But for you to reach this goal, to be confident in your decisions and choices in life, and to handle the situations that life throws at you with grace, you need to be willing to put in the effort, to try and then try again until you succeed. With this new information and insight, you'll be able to achieve these goals and take everything you've learned with you as you progress through life. You'll be a stronger, more resilient you. You'll be the person you want to be—on your own terms, without the world interfering, because you'll be the one in charge of how you handle life's curveballs and how you slay and conquer the challenges you'll face every day.

Part 1: Let's Get Started

Chapter 1: How to Use This Book

Dialectical means the existence of opposites. In DBT, people are taught two seemingly opposite strategies: acceptance…and change. — CAMH

In DBT, when we talk about two opposing strategies, the first is acceptance. Acceptance is about understanding your experiences, and realizing that your behavior is valid. In contrast to acceptance, there is change, the positive changes that we make to manage our emotions better and move forward. Even though these are two opposite strategies, they complement each other in such a complex and unique way that they bring about a better understanding of your emotions, feelings, and self.

Stages of DBT

Within DBT, there are four stages that a person works through. Each stage has its own specific goals and skills that it focuses on. At the end of all four stages, the result is the ability to have a deeper meaning of life and happiness. Our focus will be on the first two stages of DBT, but for interest sake, here is a brief overview of the four stages and what each stage represents and focuses on.

Stage 1: In this stage, you feel miserable and unhappy, and it seems like you have no control over your own behavior. You might engage in reckless and risky behaviors that are damaging to yourself and the relationships you have with others. You feel like life is hell and that you can't escape what you are feeling or going through.

The goals of this stage are to move away from feeling like you are out of control, like you cannot control your behavior, and instead move toward learning to control your behavior, impulses, and feelings to regain the control you feel you have lost.

Stage 2: When you feel miserable, distressed, in pain, hopeless, or down, you start behaving in ways that are reckless because you are trying to feel in control of something. It feels like you are being punished for your feelings or suffering because your emotions aren't being recognized. Perhaps someone said that what you are feeling is just a silly teenage phase, but you know that it's not. Or, maybe you've experienced something traumatic which has left a lasting impression on you, and you can't seem to shake it off.

In short, this stage focuses on your inability to experience what you are feeling or going through without feeling anxious, nervous, uncomfortable, uneasy, or even embarrassed.

Stage 2's goal is to help you move away from avoiding these emotions or suffering with them and into experiencing these emotions and learning to understand that it is important to experience all emotions, even if they aren't comfortable. Experiencing emotions is about acknowledging what you feel and understanding that it's alright to feel what you feel—just don't dwell on these emotions. Instead, feel them in the moment and then let them pass.

Stage 3: Life is about living and not just about surviving until the next day. In this stage, the focus is on moving from only surviving, pushing through the challenging moments, toward enjoying and living life to its fullest. This stage includes setting life goals for yourself, building up your self-respect, and finding peace and happiness within your life.

The goal is to learn that life will not always be filled with happiness, but that there will be painful moments too—and you need to experience these moments, work through them, and move on from them. Ultimately, it is about learning to let go of the negative things and experience life to its fullest, even when you fall on hard times.

Stage 4: For some, this stage is needed; for others, their journey through DBT ends at stage 3. Stage 4 was specifically created for those who feel that they need more than a life of happiness and unhappiness, and recognize that they need more in life to feel fulfilled. They crave a deeper connection to the world around them. This stage is about finding deeper meaning in the experiences of life and often involves a deeper spiritual connection.

The goal here is to move away from feeling incomplete and toward experiences that allow a person to experience more joy and freedom.

It's also important to know that these stages don't always move from Stage 1 to Stage 2 and then to Stage 3; some stages may be repeated, or you might move from Stage 1 to Stage 2 and back to Stage 1. This is because the skills you will learn from DBT are skills you will carry with you, and as you experience new challenges in life, you might find yourself having to repeat certain stages.

This does not mean you are moving backward or aren't making process; it simply means that you are experiencing life for what it is: a rollercoaster ride with ups and downs, happiness and unhappiness, with easy moments and challenging moments. Life in its fullest is about experiencing everything, even when it's uncomfortable, even if we don't want to feel it or go through it. You cannot know what happiness feels like unless you've experienced a little unhappiness. You won't understand the importance of a smile or happiness unless you've experienced the opposite too.

The Four Modules and Exercises

Our focus is on the first two stages of DBT and on the four modules of DBT: namely, core mindfulness, distress tolerance, interpersonal effectiveness, and emotion regulation. This book is therefore divided into four parts to represent each of the four modules of DBT.

In each part, we will discuss and define the concepts and terms related to each module. We will also define and discuss the skills related to each module and provide an exercise or worksheet to work through. Of these exercises and worksheets, you'll encounter two different types: The first is "Worksheets for Teens". These exercises can be done by you alone, so you will not need an authority figure (such as a parent, teacher, or other adult you trust) to help you work through these exercises. The other activities are "Worksheets for Parents/Teachers". You won't be able to do these alone as you will need a parent or teacher who you trust to help guide you through these activities. They are designed to help you deeper understand the activities that you've already done by yourself. Think of these activities as a way to reinforce what you'll be learning on your own.

Can I Do DBT Alone?

Now for the question, you've been waiting to have answered: Can you do DBT alone? While it's not an easy 'yes' or 'no' answer, it is possible. While it can be challenging to learn DBT skills independently, it's not impossible. But fair warning, you might experience moments where the content will feel overwhelming, and that's okay. Most things worth learning take time and aren't easy, but they are well worth it!

Consider a few things when doing DBT by yourself: Firstly, create a set time for yourself each day or once a week to work through the content of this book so as to ensure you stay motivated; secondly, find a quiet place where you can read and do your exercises to stay focused; and lastly, practice these skills within situations, or with friends or family if you're confident enough. Remember to take your time and move at a pace that is comfortable for you.

In summary, this book and its worksheets are designed to be completed independently or with the help of a parent or teacher, making it possible to practice DBT in the comfort of your own space and with a companion. It's important to note that this is just the beginning of your journey to learn and apply DBT skills in your everyday life.

Chapter 2: The ABCs of DBT

*DBT acknowledges the **need for change in a context of acceptance of situations and recognizing the constant flux of feelings**—many of them contradictory—without having to get caught up in them.* —Dialectical Behavioral Therapy

Now that we understand what to expect from this book, it's time to learn what Dialectical Behavior Therapy (DBT) is, why it's considered a subtype of Cognitive Behavioral Therapy (CBT), and everything else in between.

What is DBT?

In its simplest form, DBT is a type of behavioral therapy that acknowledges that life is complex and can cause intense, negative emotions but that also understands that positive and helpful behavioral changes are needed to overcome them. In its more complex form, DBT focuses on bringing two opposing forces together, allowing them to coexist and keeping them in balance. In other words, when you're feeling intense, negative emotions that push you towards behaving a certain way, you need to accept that these emotions are valid and that it's okay to feel them, but on the other hand, you also need to understand that the behavior these emotions are pushing you toward is not helpful or healthy.

In short, DBT is a treatment that focuses on teaching you to cope with life, deal with your emotions, maintain healthy relationships, and live in the moment rather than getting stuck in dwelling on the past or in worries about the future.

Where Did DBT Come From?

DBT was initiated by a woman named Marsha Linehan, who was focused on creating a treatment that would help women who struggled with social or emotional problems (and often a combination of the two) and were suicidal. Through science, practice, and clinical experiences, Linehan created a treatment that helped patients accept themselves, their emotions, thoughts, the world, and those around them. This treatment focused on using change-oriented strategies. Thus it became a dialectical therapy (a therapy that combines two opposing ideas or forces).

The Four Modules

As we've hinted at in the previous chapter, our focus is on the four modules of DBT. In each module, you'll learn and gain new skills for coping with your intense emotions.

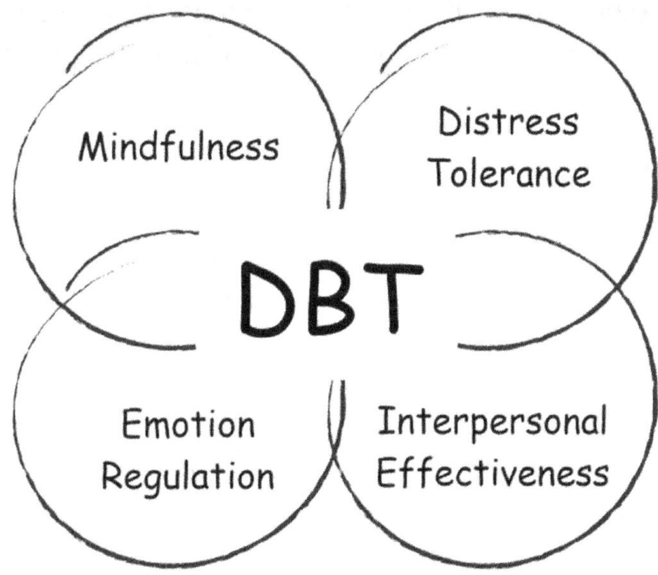

Your first skill is **mindfulness**. Mindfulness is a skill that helps you cope better with the things that trigger stress for you. Within this module, you'll learn about accepting the situations and experiences around you. You'll learn to live in the present moment and challenge the negative things you think or say about yourself. The ultimate goal of this skill is to develop your Wise Mind.

The second skill is **distress tolerance**. You will experience painful and overwhelming moments; learning distress tolerance will help you develop the skills and mechanisms to face emotional pain. This skill also teaches you how to stay away from the pain until you are ready to deal with it. In this module, you'll learn acceptance and grounding techniques, as well as how to act with intention rather than function merely on auto-pilot.

The third skill is **emotion regulation**. This section will focus on teaching you skills that involve accepting all your emotions, whether positive or negative, and checking to see whether what you are feeling is real or is a triggered emotion that's brought up because of external factors. During this section, you'll also learn that your emotions might lie to you and that the opposite action is needed when this happens. Like distress tolerance, this module will also encourage you to be intentional in your actions.

The final skill is **interpersonal effectiveness**. It's a bit of a mouthful, but this section aims to teach you how to cultivate self-respect, improve and maintain relationships, and get what you want. In other words, it's about teaching you how to care for yourself by speaking up about your own needs, setting healthy boundaries, and respecting yourself.

All in all, the skills that each of these four modules will teach you and guide you through are skills you'll be using every day, and in many different situations you might face. Learning these skills while you are still a teenager and struggling with these intense emotions as you develop and grow will help you live a more fulfilling life as an adult and cope better with the struggles and challenges you'll face later in life.

Who is DBT For?

DBT, while primarily focused on those who struggle with borderline personality disorder, is effective in helping those who struggle with:

- anxiety

- depression

- eating disorders

- attention-deficit/hyperactivity disorder (ADHD)

- obsessive compulsive disorder (OCD)

- post-traumatic stress disorder (PTSD)

- substance use disorder

- bipolar disorder

DBT is effective in treating the above conditions because each of these conditions has an element in them that is centered around having unhealthy or problematic coping strategies to control intense, negative emotions. DBT helps you learn healthier ways to cope rather than relying on your previouslu learned behaviors while trying to simultaneously push through these intense, negative emotions.

For this very reason, DBT is an excellent form of therapy for teens who are going through the motions of growing up. Teenagers are at a point in their lives where they feel vulnerable, worried, scared, and emotional because not only are their bodies going through significant changes, but their minds and emotions are too.

What is CBT?

Cognitive behavioral therapy (CBT), much like DBT, is a type of psychotherapy. It's based on the principle that negative actions or feelings result from one's own distorted beliefs and thoughts and not due to past events that are unconsciously at work. CBT is a combination of cognitive and behavioral therapy, where the first focuses on your moods and thoughts, and the second focuses on your actions and behaviors.

CBT aims to help you develop more constructive and helpful ways to react to things that cause you stress. The goal is that you will learn to cope and recover from stressful situations by managing unwanted behaviors. In short, CBT focuses on how your thoughts, feelings, and behaviors influence each other and includes techniques that concentrate on finding perspective, problem-solving, re-evaluation, and self-recognition.

We've briefly mentioned CBT because DBT is a subtype of CBT. DBT is built upon the building blocks that CBT had already laid down. And as it is a subtype, there is some overlap in the focuses of these treatments. Both therapies focus on helping you better understand yourself and manage your thoughts and behaviors.

DBT vs CBT: The Crucial Difference

But just as they are similar in some aspects, DBT and CBT have some significant differences:

- While DBT is based on CBT, DBT puts a lot more emphasis on managing your emotions and maintaining your relationships with others.

- CBT allows you to recognize when your thoughts or beliefs are the problem and helps you redirect unhelpful thoughts, whereas DBT aims to help patients find ways to accept who they are, feel safe, and manage their emotions to reduce destructive or harmful behaviors.

- CBT focuses on specific relationships, and DBT focuses on the patient's interpersonal connection with family, friends, and romantic partners. It deliberately teaches ways to deal with intense emotional responses in relationships.

- DBT teaches you how to accept your situations or experiences and understand that what you are experiencing is in fact real. CBT focuses on your goals and developing skills to help you solve problems and change your thoughts, feelings, and behaviors.

- The most significant difference is their approach to treatment. While CBT focuses on your thinking patterns and behaviors, DBT focuses on how you interact with yourself, others, and the world around you.

Even though these therapies have different approaches, goals, and focus points, neither treatment is better than the other. Rather, the choice between them is dependent on preference and your end goal. Our focus is on DBT because it focuses on self, others, and the world and is centered around strong, intense emotions—often the cause of many of the anxieties we experience.

Benefits of DBT

DBT's benefits are possibly the most significant reason you are here—it's the results you are looking for and working towards. DBT has many benefits. Here are a few of the most common ones:

- It will **improve your relationships** with others. Because DBT focuses on yourself, others, and the world around you, it will teach you how to improve and maintain your relationships with others.

- It **improves your quality of life**. When you learn that it's okay to find certain situations or things difficult, you'll be more at ease when you start making small changes to accept these difficult situations and learn to respond to them better.

- You'll be able to **regulate your emotions**. DBT skills will help you stop reacting impulsively to the emotions you are experiencing but will rather teach you to take a moment, check your emotions, and respond more calmly to these emotions rather than in a destructive manner.

- You'll **have a better understanding of yourself and your emotions and thoughts**. The skills and strategies that DBT teaches you will help you understand what you are experiencing and help you work through these emotions or thoughts and find ways to adapt your automatic responses to negative emotions by learning healthy responses.

- The **skills go beyond mental illness**. While DBT is focused on mental health conditions, the skills that are taught can be used in other areas of your life too. They aren't just focused on helping you improve your quality of life as a teenager, but they can be carried with you into your adult life where you'll face new and different challenges and experiences.

- You'll be able to **maintain positive thoughts and behaviors** because DBT focuses on accepting situations and learning positive and healthy ways to respond to these circumstances or situations. These small changes will be carried through to the next experience or challenge, and it will become easier to maintain these positive thoughts and behaviors.

Now that you know all there is to know about both DBT and CBT, the specific benefits of DBT, you have a clearer idea of what you'll encounter as you work through this book. It's time that we take that first step and start our DBT journey with mindfulness.

Part 2: Core Mindfulness

Chapter 3: Here and Now, What and How

When I was first told I had BPD I remembered feeling scared. The name 'personality disorder' made me feel like there was something wrong with who I am as a person. —
Loren

Life can be overwhelming, with constant distractions from social media notifications, messages, and more. Stress and anxiety have become a normal part of everyday life. However, there is a way to find calm in the chaos and slow down: it's called mindfulness.

Mindfulness: Focus on the Present

Mindfulness is about intentionally observing your present moment and staying away from worrying about the past and the future. Think of mindfulness as being aware of your thoughts, feelings, surroundings, and even your bodily sensations. In essence, it's about rooting yourself in the here and now rather than having your mind fly off to worry about things that have already happened or things that are to come.

The word 'mindfulness' means to have clear comprehension, and if we go down the rabbit hole, "clear comprehension" refers to understanding something clearly. Therefore mindfulness is about clearly understanding each moment of your experience, having a clear understanding of what you are feeling and thinking, and understanding why you're feeling certain feelings or having certain thoughts in a given situation. Once you are able to live in every moment with a clear understanding of what you're experiencing, you will start to realize that the worries—the anxieties—that you experience throughout the day are about your mind searching for stimulation and finding it by thinking of new things and situations, or by simply finding new ways to check out of reality.

This is all part of your mind's nature—it wants to think, analyze, and figure things out. It's a toddler who is excitedly exploring everything—but trying to do it all at once. Therefore, mindfulness is about taking your mind's toddler ways and gently shifting them, and teaching your mind to settle down, breathe, and experience the present moment. Mindfulness is about you taking control of your mind and gently teaching it that living in the present moment is better because then we don't get caught up in the anxieties of the past or future but rather enjoy the here and now.

We think it's worth mentioning one thing: Mindfulness doesn't involve having a mind that is full. Instead, it involves using every part of your mind to its fullest to experience and understand the *present* moment. A full mind is one that's filled with the past, the present, and the future. When your mind is full, it causes you to feel anxious, worried, overwhelmed, angry, irritated, and numb because there's too much going on, and you're struggling to calm the raging sea and be in the present.

Accepting the Present Moment

Being mindful fosters calm, openness, understanding, and non-judgmental thinking. When you practice mindfulness, you're teaching yourself (and your mind) how to be calm during stressful situations, such as exams. It also teaches you to become more focused when you need to do something hard or complicated, such as studying for an exam or improving a skill, or even something as simple as cleaning your room. The other reason why mindfulness is important is that it will help you be less impulsive in your actions, and teach you to be more aware of your emotions and thoughts, all while enabling you to regulate your emotions better. It will also help you have a better overall outlook on life and more confidence in who you are.

You're still young, still learning about life and who you are, and when your mind becomes filled with the worries and anxieties of days that have passed or are yet to come, you lose sight of enjoying the world around you and the experiences that you have yet to experience. You start missing out on the wonderful moments of being a teenager (even when they aren't always wonderful) and lose sight of just enjoying life as it is instead of stealing today's happiness because you're worried about tomorrow—which is still to come and shouldn't be clouding up your present anyway!

Dwelling on things that have passed and can't be changed causes you to feel hopeless, angry, sad, or even depressed. We all want a time machine sometimes to go back in time and do things differently, but we forget that if we were to change a single moment in the past, our present would not be what it is now. That worry you have about people remembering the embarrassing moment when you spilled a drink on your lap and it looked like you peed your pants is only stuck inside your head because of the emotions it made you feel; but others have forgotten it because, like you, they worry about their own moments. Letting go of the past isn't always easy, but dwelling on the past steals the joy and happiness from our present moments.

And something that's often worse than dwelling on the past is looking to the future. That's a hole no one wants to fall through, and yet it's one we stumble into way too often. For example, the boy or girl you like said 'no' to going to the dance with you. At that moment, you feel such extreme emotions, and your mind starts forming future scenarios where you're alone, and they are happy, or you'll be laughed at for not having a date to the dance. But after going to the dance alone, you realize that maybe not having a date wasn't so bad: you got to dance with your friends, ask any girl to dance who also didn't have a date, and you realized that a lot of the people around you came alone too. All the worrying you did turns out to be for nothing. And that's why it's important that you learn the importance of mindfulness and understand the harm that dwelling on the past or looking to the future can have on your happiness, your feelings, thoughts, and outlook on life.

That being said, it's important that we look into the two-component model of mindfulness. One component focuses on teaching yourself to pay attention to your present moment and to be involved in the current experience. At the same time, the other component focuses on adopting acceptance and openness toward your experiences. In short, the components of mindfulness are about paying attention to the experiences of the present moments but also understanding that you need to be open and accepting of the experience—even when it's not what you expected.

Mindfulness-Informed Interventions

Where mindfulness-based interventions (MBIs) focus on formal meditation to foster mindfulness skills, mindfulness-informed interventions (MIIs) focus on incorporating mindfulness practices through non-meditation-based techniques to develop mindfulness skills. MIIs use stories, metaphors, and experiential exercises to promote mindfulness rather than using meditation practices. For this reason, we've focused on MIIs because learning to meditate takes intense focus, concentration, and practice that most teenagers don't have time for due to their busy school, sport, and social schedules. Meditation is also difficult to do without a guide, when you have too much energy or negative biases—which most of us have, whether teenagers or adults by the way! The result will be the same whether using meditation-based or informed mindfulness practices. Both of these practices will foster mindfulness, reducing your negative thinking patterns and reactions to events, situations, and challenges and increasing your focus, attention, and compassion towards yourself and others.

DBT is, therefore, a prime example of MIIs because you do not need to learn how to meditate, and you'll still gain all the skills and benefits. These skills are also transferable to everyday situations, rather than needing to find a quiet place to meditate to benefit from the same outcomes as those you'll be learning without meditation. The ultimate goal you'll be working towards when practicing mindfulness is to develop what is known as a "Wise Mind". In order to develop and use your Wise Mind, you'll need to learn the 'what' and the 'how' skills.

Mindfulness Skills: The What and the How

So what are these 'what' and 'how' skills? Firstly, 'what' skills refer to the things you do to cope with the situations you face, and 'how' skills refer to how you cope. Secondly, there are three types of 'what' and 'how' skills: 'What' skills involve **observing**, **describing**, and **participating**; the three 'how' skills involve being **non-judgmental**, doing things **one-mindfully**, and being **effective**.

Once you are able to understand and practice these six skills, you will be able to develop and start to use your Wise Mind.

The Wise Mind

But what is a "Wise Mind"? It's a combination of your emotional and logical mind. Your Wise Mind combines and balances your emotions and reasoning so that you are able to clearly and mindfully experience the moments in your life.

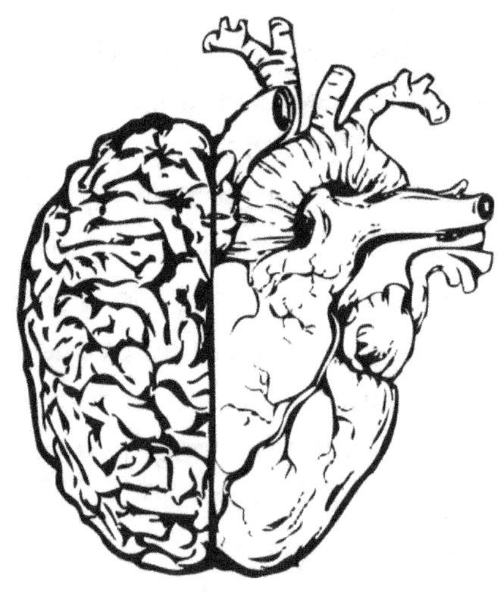

Let's start with your emotional mind: This is a state of mind where your emotions control your thoughts and actions. When this happens, it becomes difficult to think logically, plan, find the truth, or keep the situation rational rather than blow it out of proportion. When you're in this state of mind, it's often said that you're being hot-headed because when emotions run high and are intense, our behavior matches these intense feelings.

Examples of being in this state of mind are fighting with someone because you disagree, being impulsive with a trip or purchase, snapping at your parents or a friend because they didn't react or respond in the way you expected them to—or it can even be cuddling your dog or cat, or doing something because it fills you with happiness or excitement.

On the other hand, your rational mind is when your emotions aren't the controlling force. Instead, this state of mind is when you think logically and you're able to be rational and reasonable about the situation. In this state, your analytical and empirical thinking is strong, and your behavior is defined as being cool and calm. In this state, you take a rational approach to solving problems.

For example, you look up the schedule for the bus before going to wait for it, you plan your trips well in advance, you calmly talk to your friends or parents when faced with a disagreement, you study for a test. It can also be simple tasks like measuring out the ingredients when baking cookies or reading the instructions before using the new electronic toy you bought.

Learning mindfulness is crucial because it helps you stay calm during difficult situations, and allows you to enjoy life to the fullest and have a positive outlook on life. The goal of mindfulness practice is to develop and use your Wise Mind in everyday situations, which will help you cope better with challenges and react calmly. The upcoming chapters will teach you the necessary skills to achieve this state of mind.

Chapter 4: The What Skills

According to a survey, ninety-six percent of the 3,000 participants admitted that they were living on autopilot. —Marks & Spencer

Living on autopilot means going through the motions of daily life without being fully present. It's important to be aware of our choices and decisions because they shape our experiences. For example, thinking about brushing your teeth: You probably do it out of habit, but can you remember the specific details of the experience? When we live on autopilot, we lose awareness of the present moment and our experiences.

What Skills

You probably know about the 'what' skills: observe, describe, and participate. But why are they called 'what' skills? They're called that because they help you take control of your thoughts and feelings by focusing on specific actions. In short, they help you practice mindfulness. These skills will teach you to observe what's happening without labeling it, describe what you're feeling or experiencing, and participate in the experience. We'll be focusing on these three skills and discussing them in-depth, as well as providing you with techniques and exercises to practice them in your daily life.

Observing

When you observe mindfully, you're not just casually noticing things around you; instead, you're intentionally focusing on something and experiencing it with your thoughts, feelings, and senses, both within and outside of yourself.

Learning to observe may be challenging initially: your thoughts may wander, or you may find it hard to stay still during the exercise. This is normal since you're teaching your mind something new, and it takes time to acquire any new skill. Observing will help you become more mindful and aware of the world, and it will teach you how to focus and pay attention. You may feel distracted and lose focus while practicing observing, but with continued practice, you'll find it easier to pay attention and become less distracted. Impatience during the exercise is another issue you may encounter, which is a sign that you're trying to rush through it. Accept your impatience and gently bring your attention back to observing. This exercise can help you become more focused by training your mind to pay attention for five minutes daily, which will teach your brain to apply this skill to other everyday situations, resulting in increased productivity and reduced stress and anxiety.

Observation Exercise

When observing, imagine your mind as a non-stick pan. Every thought, feeling, and sensation you observe is like an egg getting fried up: You observe it and then let it slide right out of the pan. This is called the "Teflon mind". If this analogy doesn't work for you, consider these:

- You're a security guard standing at the front of a store. You're simply watching the people walk in and walk out. You are not stopping every person and asking them why they are there or how long they intend to stay.

- You're out in the park near a stream. It's autumn, and many leaves float past you in the stream. You sit down and watch the leaves float by, but you do not reach for or try to grab them. Instead, you're simply watching them come and go.

Worksheet for Teens: Observe an Object

Duration: 5 minutes, three times a week.

We are going to guide you through the practice of observing. This is an exercise that you can do by yourself and doesn't require the guidance of a parent or teacher. This worksheet has four steps that we will be guiding you on. If possible, grab a pen and paper and have it nearby. You'll be using this during the final step. If you're ready and comfortable, let's get started.

For clarification, when we refer to being non-judgmental and not judging your thoughts, we refer to how you feel toward your wandering thoughts. This means not getting angry, annoyed, irritated, or upset when you're mind wanders. Instead, take a deep breath, accept that these thoughts will come and go, and return your focus to the exercise.

Step 1: Find a Quiet and Comfortable Space

Find a calm and quiet area without any distractions. Take a few deep breaths, allowing each breath to expand your chest and stomach, which can help release any tension and promote relaxation.

Step 2: Find an Object and Focus Your Attention

Choose an everyday object in the room that is neutral and doesn't hold any sentimental value or emotional significance to you. Once you have the object picked out, focus on it using your senses. Start by using the following prompts to guide you:

- What does it look like?

- Does it have a smooth or textured surface?

- Is it round, or does it have edges?

- Is it a small or big object?

- Is it heavy or light?

- When you run your fingers over the object, what do you feel?

- Does it make a sound, or is it silent?

- Does it have a smell?

- Does it have vibrant colors?

- Is it something you can taste?

- Can you imagine the taste?

As you concentrate on the object, your mind will inevitably wander, connecting with what you observe whether emotionally or rationally. Rather than resisting your wandering thoughts, gently guide your attention back to the object. Avoid judging yourself or your thoughts for wandering; it is natural, and with continued practice, your mind will wander less frequently.

Step 3: Notice and Accept Any Experiences That Might Come Up

While observing the object, it's normal to experience different reactions and feelings, including boredom. Accept the physical sensations and emotions you feel, and then return your focus to the object. Don't get caught up in analyzing why you feel a certain way. Simply notice the sensations and let them pass.

Step 4: Keep Track of Your Progress

After completing the exercise, jot down all your observations and experiences. Tracking your progress will allow you to easily observe how your thoughts and experiences have settled down over time.

Recreate the table below and fill in the information on the piece of paper you have kept beside you. Keep this page somewhere safe and add to it every time you do this exercise.

Date	Object	Qualities of the Object	Thoughts, Emotions, and Sensations
17 June	ball	<ul><li>small, soft, smooth</li><li>hard to squeeze</li><li>bounces</li><li>makes a soft thud</li><li>yellow</li></ul>	I realized I felt tired. Thought about what to eat for lunch. Wanted to bounce the ball. Felt my attention increase.

Describing

Describing is about giving words to what you are observing. It is about labeling your experiences without judgment. When you describe events or experiences with words, you develop the ability to label your environment and behaviors as well. This ability to describe what you are feeling will help you observe more clearly the connection between your self and your environment. Using observe and describe together will help you stay in the present moment and focus better on what you are doing rather than being on autopilot.

Labeling your thoughts and emotions teaches you how to communicate and manage them. When we are able to label our emotions and thoughts, we can understand them. But one vital aspect of labeling your thoughts and emotions is knowing they aren't facts; having a thought or feeling about something doesn't make it a fact. For example, if you feel like no one likes you or that you are unlovable, these thoughts do not make them true. They are just thoughts and just feelings. Remember that it is valid to have these real feelings, but they are not facts.

Describing Exercise

During describing exercises, it's important to keep a few things in mind and follow some tips. You can practice describing during everyday activities, like washing the dishes or going for a walk. While doing the activity, describe what you are doing and observe using your senses. Avoid being judgmental. Initially, it may be challenging not to judge the thoughts and feelings you are labeling. Think of the activity as sorting through a basket of small balls of different colors and sizes. Label a thought as a thought and a feeling as a feeling without getting caught up on why you feel this way or have these thoughts.

Worksheet for Teens: Mental Body Scan

Duration: 15 minutes, every day for a week.

This exercise is aimed at making you aware of your bodily sensations and the places in your body that carry tension, and at teaching you to focus on specific tasks or experiences and not get caught up in their sensations.

During this exercise, you may face some difficulties. Initially, you might find it challenging, which is normal when doing this activity for the first time. Try to relax and consider the exercise as a way to become calm and energized. If you struggle to complete the exercise, do as much as you can without feeling pressure to finish it. As with observing exercises, describing exercises will have your mind wandering a lot at the start, but as you continue to practice, these wandering thoughts will lessen. If you find yourself wandering away from the exercise, gently nudge your mind and attention back to the exercise. Lastly, this exercise will make you aware of the parts of your body that are tense, which might have gone unnoticed until now. Some of these areas will remain tense even after you've completed the exercise. That's alright, it's a normal reaction, and it's okay to feel frustrated or impatient because the tension isn't being fully released during the exercise. This means these areas of your body require a different form of release, such as working out, taking a nap, or massaging the tense area.

Focus your attention on different parts of your body. As you focus on these parts, make use of the following prompts:

- What do you feel?

- Does the area feel tense or relaxed?

- Does the area feel tired or energized?

- Does the area feel well-rested?

- Does the area feel like it needs to be stretched or worked out?

- Does the area make you feel calm or nervous?

- What sensations do you feel, and can you describe them?

- Does the area hurt?

- Are you clenching a muscle?

To prepare for this exercise, find a quiet and comfortable place to sit on a chair where you won't be interrupted. Ensure that your feet are flat on the ground. This exercise is best done with your eyes closed, so read through it before starting the mental body scan.

Step 1: Lower Body Awareness

Duration: 5 minutes.

Start with your toes. Describe to yourself what you feel. Move to the soles of your feet, towards your ankles, and up your leg. Consider the sensation of the chair against the back of your knees. Move further up towards your thighs. Can you feel the chair beneath you? Then work around your pelvic area, focusing on your buttocks and hips. How does the chair feel against these areas? What sensations are you experiencing?

Step 2: Upper Body Awareness

Duration: 5 minutes.

Start with your stomach. How does it feel? What sensations are you feeling? Notice any sensations, no matter how small. Move toward your lower back. Can you feel your back carrying the weight of your upper body? If you feel any tension in this area or any negative sensations, take a few deep breaths, engaging your chest and stomach as you do, and try to let go of these sensations.

Then move up into your chest and upper back—these areas can carry a lot of tension. Can you feel the chair? Do you feel tightness around your chest? Now bring the awareness to your fingertips, fingers, hands, wrist, and arms. Are you holding the chair, or are your hands resting in your lap? Are you resting weight on your elbows, or are they relaxed? Then move up your upper arms as you continue to describe what you are experiencing.

Step 3: Shoulders and Head Awareness

Duration: 5 minutes.

Your shoulders are often the first area where you feel great tension. In this area, you can feel painful tension build-up due to stress or anxiety, so pay attention when describing the sensations you feel in your shoulders. Are they relaxed, or have they been tense without you realizing it? Move up to your neck, continuing to describe any sensations you might feel. Focus on your chin, jaw, nose, cheeks, ears, eyes, nose, and head. What do you feel? What are you experiencing?

Step 4: Write Down Your Experiences

On a piece of paper, write down what you experienced at each of the three steps—no matter how small or insignificant you think that sensation or experience was. Take note of the areas that felt tense, how you felt before the exercise started, and how you felt once you were done. Keep track of your experiences as you continue this exercise throughout the week. If you found this exercise useful and relaxing, continue using it.

Participating

Let's talk about participation, the final skill. Participation requires complete immersion in a task rather than allowing obsessive thoughts to take over. It means disengaging from autopilot, which can give us a sense of ease and comfort in our daily routines. Unfortunately, living our lives on autopilot can be dangerous. It allows old habits and ways of thinking to govern our reactions to everyday things, and we risk forgetting what we experienced that day because we weren't participating. Additionally, we run the risk of someone else making choices for us.

Our daily routine can become so familiar that we disengage from the experience and allow auto-pilot to direct us. We often have no memory of doing the things we did on auto-pilot. However, to live our lives to the fullest, we need to participate in every task, no matter how routine. Participating means handling every situation like we are skilled in it and paying careful attention to everything we experience as we do the task. Continuously practicing participation will train your mind and yourself to keep autopilot disengaged and remain active in your life and choices.

When participating, it's important to acknowledge and observe uncomfortable feelings and experiences. Rather than avoiding them, try to understand their cause and the sensations they bring up. Once you've done this, move through the feeling and let it go, utilizing the skills you've already learned.

Participating Exercise: Turn Off Autopilot

Duration: Do this every day for a week. The amount of time is dependent on the task.

The only way for you to turn off your autopilot is to participate actively. This exercise can be done several times during the day and should be done for at least a week. Once this week has passed, you will be more aware of the tasks you do on autopilot and you will become more active in your daily activities.

Disengage Autopilot Exercise

Consider your morning routine, such as getting dressed, brushing your teeth, eating breakfast, or commuting to school. While doing these activities, are you scrolling through social media, watching videos, or listening to music? Instead of doing these activities on autopilot, immerse yourself in the activity. Concentrate on every movement of your body as you do this task. Focus on the sensations that you feel. Pay attention to what you observe, and describe what you see, hear, and feel.

Start by turning off your phone, music, or anything that can or will distract you as you are engaging in this activity.

Once you have an activity, use the following prompts to guide you in being an active participant:

- What do you see?

- What do you feel?

- What do you observe about the task?

- What do you hear?

- What do you smell?

- How do you feel?

- What sensations are you experiencing?

- Are you experiencing uncomfortable emotions?

- Can you describe what you are experiencing as you're participating in the activity?

- What can you describe?

It's important that you remain objective in the experience and don't get caught up in all the sensations of the experience. Don't fixate on the thoughts and feelings you are going through.

Example

As you board the bus to school, you usually plug in your headphones and turn up the music, letting your thoughts wander. However, today you decide to participate and turn off your phone. You start to notice things you never did before, like the newly cleaned seats and the change in bus driver. The neighborhood has changed, too, with a golden retriever running around and an elderly lady with strong perfume boarding the bus. Despite the scratchy seat and worn-down cushions, you feel comfortable and at ease, and even the bus jolting doesn't bother you as much because you understand the cause.

Interactive Element: Discussion Time

As we've mentioned, some worksheets will require the guidance of a parent or teacher. The following exercise is one of those worksheets. This worksheet is a Question and Answer exercise to help you reflect on the three exercises you've done thus far.

Worksheet for Parent/Teacher

Your child or student has practiced three exercises to help them develop 'what' skills. You will be helping them reflect on these exercises and what they have experienced. Please ensure that you provide them with a space where they can feel comfortable and open in answering these questions.

Ask them the following questions:

- Which exercise did you find to be the easiest?

- Which exercise did you find to be the hardest?

- Which exercise did you enjoy? Would you do it again, if needed?

- What did you learn from these exercises?

- What will you remember from these exercises and take with you through life?

Now that you've learned and practiced the 'what' skills of mindfulness, it is time that we move on to the next set of these skills, the 'how' skills.

Chapter 5: The How Skills

Studies show that only 2.5% of people can multitask. That means for most of us when we think we are doing multiple activities at once—we aren't! —Watson & Strayer

Many people believe they are good at multitasking, but the truth is that the possibility of being a multitasker is very low, only 1 in 50. When you think you are doing multiple tasks at once, you are actually task-switching.

How Skills

Similar to the 'what' skills, which focus on *what* you do when you practice mindfulness. The 'how' skills refer to how you take control of your feelings and thoughts or, more simply, *how* you practice mindfulness. DBT mindfulness teaches you to live in the present moment, understand yourself, identify your life goals, and determine the direction you want your life to take. It also enables you to evaluate your life without criticism and perform tasks with effectiveness and focus. The three skills emphasized in this section are non-judgmental thinking, one-mindful action, and effective action.

Non-Judgmentally

Do you consider yourself non-judgmental or judgmental? Let's consider what it means to be judgmental. 'Judgment' refers to forming an opinion about something by comparing or discerning it. For example, when we see someone sitting alone, we assume they are lonely or have no friends. When someone is being obnoxiously loud, we assume they are irritating and looking for attention. These assumptions we make, often negative, are judgments. It is in our nature as humans to judge; we judge our surroundings, environment, and experiences, those around us and ourselves. But when we judge, we create a negative environment within ourselves, leading to feelings of shame, sadness, or even guilt.

Taking a non-judgmental stance means aiming to observe what you are feeling or experiencing, noting it, and letting it go. By being non-judgmental, you give yourself the opportunity to be kind to yourself—even when having judgmental thoughts. So what do we mean by "an opportunity to be kind"? When you don't judge your thoughts and feelings, you're not taking on feelings of shame, guilt, or sadness. This means showing yourself the kindness that you would show a friend who is judging themselves negatively.

Consider this example: *I notice that I'm feeling sad*. This is an **observation**. *I notice my lips are turned down, my jaw is tense, and my eyelids are heavy. I notice I am feeling tired. I also feel like crying. I notice the uncomfortable feeling of tension in my stomach.* This is an **observation with a description**. *I feel sad. I shouldn't be feeling sad. Sadness is a bad thing. There is something wrong with me because I'm not happy.* This is a **judgment**. *Sadness is an emotion that is neither good nor bad. Just because I have these symptoms of sadness does not make me a sad person. I'm just experiencing sadness for the moment. It's okay to feel sad.* This is a **non-judgmental stance**.

When practicing non-judgment within mindfulness, your aim will be to take a non-judgmental stance when observing your thoughts and experiences. These stances will allow you to think differently about old ways, your environment, and your experiences. You'll be able to experience more objective thinking, understand your thoughts, feelings, and experiences better, and be able to treat yourself with understanding and compassion.

Non-judgment also means that you accept your thoughts and feelings and don't judge yourself on these experiences but rather come to understand that you are feeling them and that they do not define who you are.

How is Non-Judgment Different From Observation?

While observation asks you to notice what you are feeling and experiencing, non-judgment asks you to observe but to do it without labeling the feelings, thoughts, or experiences as good or bad. Do not become harsh towards yourself for having these thoughts or feelings, but rather accept that you feel and think these things and let them pass.

Non-Judgmental Exercise

When observation asks you to notice what you are feeling and experiencing, non-judgment ask you to observe but to do it without judgment and to not label the feelings, thoughts, or experiences as good or bad. Do not become harsh towards yourself for having these thoughts or feelings, but rather accept that you feel and think these things and let them pass.

For example, feeling guilty for saying 'no' to a social event can make you feel different things. You might think your friends will hate you for not going or that others will judge you. You might feel guilty because you feel obligated to do it but don't want to. Knowing and observing these thoughts and feelings can help you understand that your friends won't hate you for not going, nor will others judge you. And you might be feeling guilty because someone said something about missing you being there or that they won't have anyone else to sit with them. These are all natural feelings and experiences, but when you don't respond to them with judgment or your emotional mind, you understand that the guilt doesn't make you a bad friend, and saying 'no' doesn't make you a bad person. What you've done is set boundaries and made clear what you want. In a later chapter, we'll dive deeper into setting boundaries and establishing your needs. For now, let's look at the exercise that will help you practice non-judgment in your feelings and experiences.

Worksheet for Teens

This exercise consists of two stages: The first stage is relatively easier than the second one. In Stage One, you will focus on noting your thoughts. In Stage Two, you will note your thoughts, feelings, physical sensations, and any other experiences that might arise during the exercise. Stage Two will also help you become aware of things that distract you, things that you find important or upsetting, things that you find irrelevant or boring, and so forth.

During this exercise, you may encounter difficulties, especially if you haven't tried anything similar before. However, with practice, you can improve. If you find it too challenging or intense, try to stay in the exercise and take note of what you're becoming aware of. As you repeat the exercise, you'll find it easier to observe your thoughts. Another obstacle that may arise is objectivity. It can be challenging to remain objective when dealing with serious issues such as financial problems or depression. This exercise does not require you to focus on positive thoughts or have a completely optimistic outlook. Instead, it aims to provide clarity about the problems you are facing. Over time, you will learn that change is possible, and these problems and issues will no longer make you feel hopeless.

Mental Noting

Duration: 15 minutes, twice a week.

You will need a pen and paper and a timer or clock to keep time for this exercise. Once you have these items, find a quiet, comfortable place to sit without being distracted or interrupted.

Stage One: Mentally Noting Your Thoughts

Duration: 5 minutes.

Take a few deep breaths to relax. Once you feel more relaxed, close your eyes and try to tune into your thoughts. Initially, it may be difficult to listen to your thoughts and slow them down. Write down your thoughts on a piece of paper. Remember not to analyze or judge these thoughts; keep them short and simply jot them down on the page. Continue to write down every thought you have during these five minutes.

Your goal is to observe your thoughts without trying to control them. Imagine yourself as a researcher observing people who spend their time in the park on a Saturday afternoon. Your task is to sit on a park bench at the entrance and take note of simple things about the people entering the park. Write down simple descriptions such as "mother and daughter," "older man," "three teenage boys," "a couple," and so on. As thoughts come and go in your mind, simply notice them and write them down.

Use the following prompt to help you:

I am thinking about…

Fill in the blank as each thought enters your mind. For example, *I am thinking about* how difficult the pop quiz was during history. Or, *I am thinking about* playing online with my friends.

Stage Two: Mentally Noting Your Thoughts, Feelings, and Experiences

Duration: 10 minutes

Stage One focused solely on your thoughts. During this stage, we will concentrate on your thoughts, feelings, experiences, physical sensations, and anything else that may arise. For the next ten minutes, you will repeat what you did in Stage One but also include your observations about your feelings and experiences.

As you work through this exercise, practicing non-judgment towards your feelings and experiences as you write them down can become difficult. For example, you might feel depressed and write down: *I feel irritated. I always fight with my parents when I feel irritable.* This is an example of being judgmental towards your feelings and thoughts. Instead, say: *I notice that I'm feeling irritable. I also feel that my irritation will impact how I react toward others.*

By noting your experiences with objectivity and non-judgment, you can accept that you are feeling a certain emotion, understand that these emotions cause different reactions within you, and let these experiences pass. If you're struggling to write down your experiences, try the following prompts:

I feel [**fill in the emotion**].

I am thinking about [**fill in the thought**].

Thinking about [**fill in the thought**] makes me feel [**fill in the emotion**].

When [**fill in the event or situation**] happens, I feel [**fill in the emotion**], and I think [**fill in the thoughts**].

For example, *When I think about my teacher having yelled at me in class, it makes me feel angry. I also feel like crying. My stomach feels uneasy when I think about it.*

If you are distracted or fixating on specific experiences, take a few deep breaths and gently return your focus to the exercise. It won't be easy at first, but as you continue to practice, it will become easier to notice your experiences rather than analyze them.

One-Mindfully

To be one-mindful or do things one-mindfully means to be present and focused on a single task at a time. It involves doing a task with undivided attention and focusing on the activity with mindfulness. One-mindfulness is associated with doing something with a single mind.

Therefore, when trying to multitask, we do the opposite of one-mindfully. Most of us cannot multitask, and what we think is multitasking is actually switching between tasks. This forces our minds to jump and readjust from one task to the next, causing us to lose valuable focus and time, ultimately making multitasking ineffective.

By doing these tasks one-mindfully, we can complete them quickly without losing time and focus. Multitasking, like autopilot, can cause us to lose track of what we are doing. For instance, while watching TV and eating chips, we can finish the bag without realizing it. Similarly, watching videos on the phone while brushing our teeth can make us forget if we brushed our teeth at all. Trying to do more than one task at a time can cause us to lose focus.

If you still think multitasking is effective or a good way to manage your day-to-day tasks, consider the following proven side-effects of multitasking:

- **It lowers your IQ**. According to a study by the University of London, multitasking lowers your IQ by 15 points, bringing down your cognitive capacity to that of an eight-year-old (Bradberry, 2014).

- **It reduces the density of your brain**. According to the University of Sussex, multitasking reduces the density of certain brain regions, and these regions are responsible for your cognitive and emotional regulation and empathy (Bealing, 2014).

- **It makes you more distracted**. Switching between tasks causes your mind to constantly think about the other tasks you need to do while doing your current task. Multitasking, therefore, teaches your mind to focus on other things while you're busy with a task.

One-Mindfully Exercise

Observe, describe, and non-judgmental exercises have already taught you how to focus on one thing at a time and be present in the moment. The one-mindful exercise we will do is one you've been doing all along. You're doing it right now as you read, but we will teach you how to become aware of what you are doing. This exercise will help you calm down, reduce distracted thoughts, and relax your body. Once you become comfortable with this exercise, you can practice it anywhere.

Worksheet for Teens: Sensations of Breathing

Duration: 10 minutes, once a day for a week.

For this exercise, you will need a pen and paper and a way of keeping time. Before you start the exercise, find a quiet, comfortable place to sit where you will not be interrupted.

Think about how you feel: What is your general mood for today? Are you happy, stressed, sad, or sleepy? If you feel distracted or your attention drifts away, try closing your eyes while breathing. Start to notice what you feel when you breathe: Can you feel your chest expand? Do your shoulders move with each breath? Feel the air move into your nose, windpipe, and lungs. Can you feel the air blowing against the skin below your nose when you breathe out? What else do you feel? Are these new sensations?

Once done, take a moment to think about how you feel: Has your mood changed or stayed the same? Do you feel calmer or more relaxed? How would you describe the way you feel after the exercise?

Copy the table below and fill it in on the piece of paper after each exercise.

Date:	On a scale from 1 - 10. How distracted are you?	How did you feel BEFORE the exercise?	How did you feel AFTER the exercise?
17 June	8	anxious tired hungry	tired hungry calm

Effectively

We've all done things that can be classified as "cutting off our nose to spite our face". This often happens when we are more focused on being right or proving a point instead of focusing on what is important rather than wasting that energy doing something that won't serve us.

Consider a situation where you did something to prove a point, but it ended up hurting you as well. For instance, you and your friend are arguing about who should test your science project first. You want to go first, but your friend insists on going first to demonstrate how to do it without breaking the project. You take the project and do the first test, hoping to prove that you can do it right too, but end up breaking the project. Now, both of you need to start all over again. This is an example of an ineffective situation.

Understanding the implications of your actions is crucial for being effective. This means considering the most effective option instead of just proving a point or being right. To shift your mindset towards effectiveness, focus on what works and what can help you achieve your goals and desires in different situations, rather than concepts like right and wrong or fair and unfair. Remember that it's okay to try something else or step away from a situation if it's not working or is making you feel worse.

Effectively Exercise

This exercise builds on the non-judgmental exercise of mentally noticing your thoughts. It helps you defuse difficult situations and create space between yourself and your thoughts. The exercise teaches you to reduce your reactivity to negative thoughts, which can often lead to unproductive behavior and unnecessary suffering.

Worksheet for Parent/Teacher: Leaves in the River

Duration: 10 minutes, twice a week.

You will require the help of a parent or teacher to guide you through this exercise, unlike the previous ones. Once you feel confident in your ability to do the exercise, you can start doing it by yourself. If you have difficulty doing it alone, ask for assistance with a few more exercises and try again.

For the parent/teacher: follow these steps to guide them into the exercise, while keeping your voice low and calm.

Step 1: Visualize

To guide your child/student through this exercise, ensure they are comfortable and relaxed. Instruct them to visualize a flowing river in front of them, with autumn leaves gently drifting on the water. Add more details to enhance their visualization, such as:

- The water is clear as it rushes past.

- The air is fresh.

- The sun is warm as it shines down on you.

- The leaves floating on the water are of different colors and shapes. Some are green. Others are yellow, or red, or brown. Some are small, and others are big.

Alternatively, if seeing an image makes this easier for them, let them spend a few moments staring at the image below to start visualizing the river. Provide them with the sensory information above as they continue to picture the river and the leaves.

Step 2: Turn the Leaves Into Thoughts

Tell them to take a deep breath and focus on their thoughts. Encourage them to notice their thoughts without judgment or analysis. Ask them to visualize their thoughts as leaves floating by and to summarize each thought in one or a few words.

Then instruct them to visualize the following:

- The water is starting to flow faster. The leaves that once drifted slowly on the river are now rushing past. The leaves are there for a moment, and then they are gone.

- As each leaf flows away, so does the thought.

- As new thoughts enter your mind, a new leaf approaches and flows away.

This exercise will continue for ten minutes. If you see your child/student scrunching up their face or having difficulty visualizing or letting their thoughts go, gently help them revisualize the river by giving them the visualization details from Step 1 and Step 2.

Step 3: Completing and Noticing

Once ten minutes have passed, ask them to open their eyes and tell you how they are feeling. Ask them whether they notice anything different about how they feel now compared to when they started the exercise.

The first time they do this exercise, they might feel overwhelmed, annoyed, or discouraged because they struggled to visualize or turn their thoughts into leaves that pass them by. This is all normal. As they continue to practice and learn to visualize, it will become easier, and the exercise will leave them more relaxed.

Interactive Element: Discussion Time

Worksheet for Parent/Teacher

During this section, your child/student has participated in three exercises to help them practice the mindfulness 'how' skills. You will be helping them reflect on the exercises they have participated in. Please ensure that you provide them with a safe and comfortable space where they can feel comfortable answering the following questions:

- Which exercise did you find the easiest?

- Which exercise did you find the hardest?

- Which exercise did you enjoy, and would you do it again if needed?

- Did you find it difficult to visualize the river with the leaves in the last exercise, and what did you find challenging about it?

- What will you remember from these exercises, and what did you learn from them?

Now that you know and have practiced the six core mindfulness skills of DBT, it's time that we move on to what these skills were helping you achieve: The Wise Mind.

Chapter 6: The Wise Mind

The Wise Mind is the junction point where your emotional and rational minds overlap. It is when you react to a situation with rational thought and calm emotions instead of overly emotional or irrational ones—it's the balance between your two minds.

In all our discussions about the wise mind, we've talked about it like a physical mind. However, it is a more symbolic mind, meaning it's not a physical part of your mind that you'll be accessing. Instead, it's finding the balance between the two opposing aspects of your mind and bringing them together. Every skill you've practiced to this point has taught your emotional mind to let go of intense emotions and think before reacting while simultaneously training your rational mind to understand where your feelings are coming from. Thus, you've gathered the skills that will allow you to start practicing using your Wise Mind.

In this chapter, we will provide three activities to teach you how to start using your Wise Mind. But since this is a metaphoric state of mind and you haven't used this part of your mind before—or when you did, you weren't aware of it—here are a few signs that you're using or have used your Wise Mind. These signs will also help you know when you are using your Wise Mind going forward.

You are using your Wise Mind when:

- You feel it in your belly or gut, the center of your head, or between your eyes.

- You sense that you are stepping back from a situation.

- You make a decision and feel it is right because it doesn't fill you with dread, anxiety, or doubt.

- You have a sense of calm following a crisis or difficult situation.

- You grasp the full picture of a situation instead of only seeing parts like before.

- You feel reluctant because you may want a different answer or for the situation to be easier and less painful, but you know deep inside what the truth is.

- Your spontaneous decision seems right to you.

- You can finally understand something that has puzzled you for a long time.

Remember that everyone experiences their Wise Mind differently, and the experiences mentioned above might differ from what you experience when using your Wise Mind. In Activity 1, we will dive into how you will know when you're using your Wise Mind and when you're not.

Worksheet for Teens

The following activities will focus on combining and using the skills you've learned to engage your Wise Mind and train it to become the mind you activate when faced with emotionally charged or challenging situations.

You will need a pen and paper and a quiet and comfortable space to do these activities.

Activity 1: The Wise Mind

Duration: 10 minutes, three times a week.

Your Wise Mind is an extraordinary tool that can help you find guidance for your problems, doubts, and confusion. When you feel stuck, not knowing which way to go because you feel too emotional or too rational about a situation, this exercise that engages your Wise Mind will lead you toward the solution.

Your Wise Mind sits in the overlap between your emotional mind and your rational mind. When you are in your emotional mind, you're feelings control your thoughts and behaviors. And when you're in your rational mind, your thoughts and behaviors are controlled by your logical reasoning. And in the middle of these two minds sits your Wise Mind that combines your two minds into one that can recognize and accept your feelings while making you rationally respond to them. The Venn diagram below visually represents where your Wise Mind sits between your rational and emotional mind.

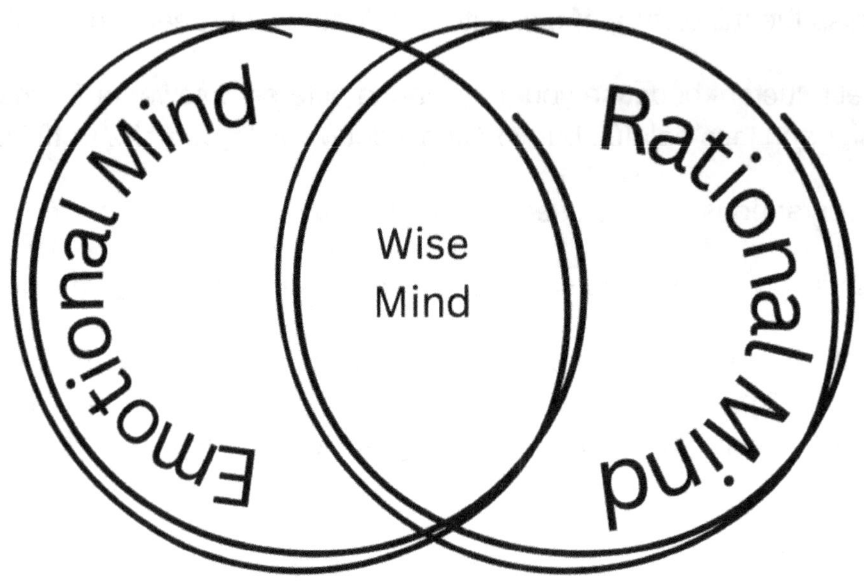

Step 1: Think About a Problem

Take a few deep breaths and focus on how each breath expands your chest and stomach, helping you relax. Now, think of a problem or situation that has been bothering you and allow yourself a few minutes to reflect. What is causing you to feel anxious, worried, or unhappy? Let your thoughts and feelings guide you to this problem. Once you have identified the problem, gently observe it.

Step 2: Use Your Wise Mind

You will observe this problem for five minutes and ask your Wise Mind for guidance by picking one of the two methods below:

Method 1: While engaging your Wise Mind, ask it a question about your problem. Listen patiently. Do not attempt to answer the question yourself; instead, rely on your intuition. What does your intuition tell you about this problem and its solution? If you receive an answer, do not act on it. Observe the answer without judgment and be aware of the response you received. If you did not receive an answer, that is perfectly okay. As you continue this exercise, you will become more familiar with how to get an answer from your Wise Mind.

Method 2: Sometimes, in challenging situations or when faced with a problem, we may not know what to ask our Wise Mind. This method involves focusing on the situation and allowing your Wise Mind to provide an answer or solution to your unasked question. Repeat this exercise until the time runs out. If you receive an answer or solution, observe it without judgment and accept what your Wise Mind has made you aware of. If you don't receive an answer or solution, that's okay. With continued practice, you'll learn how to engage your Wise Mind.

Am I Using My Wise Mind?

Consider whether you were objective about the situation or problem when you got the answer. Were you clouded by emotions or ignoring them? If you find yourself ignoring emotions, being clouded by them, or unable to be objective, you're not engaging your Wise Mind; instead, you're engaging either your rational or emotional mind. Observe what is coming to the surface during these moments and notice if there is something you can learn from these thoughts or feelings.

Activity 2: 7-Day Deep Dive

Duration: 15 minutes, every day for a week.

This exercise can help you find clarity in your emotions. Regularly doing this exercise can improve your ability to recognize your emotions, leading to better control over your behavior. You can also learn to separate yourself from situations until you can think through them and respond with clarity and calm.

Step 1: Pick Your Emotion

As you sit there, is there a specific emotion you are feeling? It can be either positive or happy. If you're being negatively overwhelmed by one emotion, focus on an emotion you felt earlier. Pick one from the list below if you can't pick an emotion. Focus on an emotion you've recently experienced so that you can tap into the moment you felt that emotion.

POSITIVE	NEGATIVE
	Angry
Blissful	Bored
Bubbly	Confused
Content	Disappointed
Curious	Embarrassed
Delightful	Empty
Determined	Enraged
Eager	Envious
Excited	Exhausted
Happy	Frustrated
Hopeful	Guilty
Joyful	Hopeless
Lively	Hurt
Loved	Indifferent
Loving	Insecure
Pleased	Irritated
Proud	Jealous
Relaxed	Lonely
Relieved	Nervous
Respected	Regretful
Safe	Restless
Satisfied	Sad
Secure	Scared
Smart	Shy
Strong	Upset
	Vulnerable

Step 2: Draw Your Emotion

Take a moment to think about what your emotion looks like and then draw the emotion on a piece of paper. It doesn't matter how your picture looks as long as it makes sense to you. Be as detailed as possible about the emotion you are feeling or focusing on. For example, you might draw a bed if you feel tired or draw a lock to represent how you feel safe. It doesn't matter what you draw as long as it's a picture that visually represents what you feel and makes sense to you.

Step 3: What Action Is Your Emotion?

Think about your emotion. What action do you associate with this emotion? When you think about this feeling, what do you want to do to act on this emotion? Describe this action on a piece of paper. Be as descriptive as you can be. For example, if you feel irritated, you might feel like screaming, slamming a door, or hiding in your room. If you feel happy, maybe you feel like dancing, singing, or doing something silly.

Step 4: Your Emotion's Intensity

On the paper, write down how intensely you feel this emotion on a scale of one to ten, with ten being the most intense. If you struggle to define your emotion's intensity using the scale, find a way to describe the intensity creatively. For example, anger might be lava when it's at ten and boiling water when it's eight. Think of how you could explain the intensity of that emotion and write it down.

Step 5: Write Your Thoughts

Now that you've identified, drawn, and described your emotion, consider what thoughts this emotion has brought up in you. Be careful not to confuse a thought with another emotion. Try not to use words that are listed above. For example, you feel alone, and your thoughts are about a friend you haven't talked to in a while. Or perhaps you thought about watching a movie to make the feeling lessen.

It's important to note that everyone experiences this activity differently. For some, the creativity of the activity is engaging. For others, it might not be easy to be creative. If you struggle with creativity, try using words or some other form of description until you feel comfortable being creative. But, if possible, follow the instructions even if they don't make sense. They will start to make sense later.

Activity 3: Turn Judgment to Non-Judgment

Duration: 10 minutes, three times a week.

When you do this activity, there will be times when it's easy for you to write down your feelings and thoughts, but there will also be times when you struggle. That's alright. Try to do your best.

Step 1: Write It All Down

Take a few deep breaths and think about a recent experience you had. On the piece of paper, write down what your feelings and thoughts were about this experience. Continue to do this until you have about three to five experiences written down, being factual and honest about your feelings and thoughts.

Step 2: Change Them to Non-Judgment

Look at the first experience, and notice where you were judgmental with your thoughts or feelings. Now rewrite this experience into one that is non-judgmental and focuses on only the facts of the experience, taking your emotions into account and considering why you felt the way you did.

Here are a few examples:

Judgment: I can't stand it when my little brother screams. I want to scream at my parents for not doing anything about it.
Mindful Form: I can hear my little brother scream. I feel angry and irritated because my parents don't make him stop. I feel they shouldn't allow him to continue his screaming when he's upset.

Judgment: I feel stupid. I failed another test, and now I don't have a future.
Mindful Form: I feel disappointed and sad because I failed a test. I think I am stupid, but I am not. I was ill-prepared for the test. This one test does not define my future. I will have a future, no matter my test scores.

The three activities mentioned above emphasize the use of mindfulness to cultivate your Wise Mind and apply it when necessary. It may take some time and effort to master the skill, but once you do, you can utilize your Wise Mind and these techniques in your daily life.

Each skill you've learned so far has taught you mindfulness and the benefits of being mindful in your everyday life. Mindfulness allows you to let go of past worries and future anxieties and live in the present moment. You become aware of your experiences, emotions, and thoughts that impact how you feel about your life. You learn to adapt and change them so that you can accept these feelings and let them go. Mindfulness teaches you to stay calm, collected, and wise when faced with emotionally overwhelming situations.

Part 3: Distress Tolerance

Chapter 7: Dealing With Overwhelming Emotions

Distress tolerance skills enable us to survive immediate crises without making things worse and to accept reality when we can't change it, and it's not what we want it to be. — Marsha Linehan

Have you ever been in a crisis and wished there were instructions on getting through it? Perhaps you need a survival guide for when situations become difficult. While not a guide, distress tolerance skills are skills that will help you survive the stressful and distressing moments in your life.

What Is Distress Tolerance?

Distress is the pain and suffering you feel in your body and mind when experiencing a painful situation. Tolerance, however, refers to your ability to endure the painful situation or the suffering and pain you feel inside your body and mind. In the context of DBT, distress tolerance refers to your ability to cope with an emotionally distressing situation, whether real or perceived. But it also involves your ability to endure this situation without worsening it.

Our lives are filled with stressful moments, some small and some big. Some we can manage without prolonging the pain and suffering, and others might leave us swimming through troubled waters as we struggle to get through them.

An Emphasis on Acceptance

Distress tolerance is not about changing the situation, pushing it away, or burying it so deep that you think it will never come to the surface again. No, it's about accepting the reality of the situation and not demanding that it change. When you work against the environment of your distress and refuse to accept the situation, thought, or emotion for what it is, you are prolonging the pain, which results in you suffering unnecessarily. But, when you accept the situation for what it is, you aren't prolonging the pain or causing yourself more suffering; instead, you experience the ordinary pain associated with the situation.

It's important to know that acceptance is not agreeing to what is happening; acceptance is learning that you cannot *control* the situation, so you *accept* that the situation is what it is. But it's also knowing that when you accept the situation for what it is, you can react without being impulsive or destructive.

Distress tolerance skills will help you lower the intensity of the emotional pain you experience. The process of learning these skills will teach you to cope more effectively in distressing situations and positively change how you handle these difficult situations, thoughts, and emotions. In short, distress tolerance skills will help you survive crises through practicing the skills before the crisis occurs. We will focus on three distress tolerance skills that will help you incorporate acceptance into your everyday life.

ACCEPTS

Distress tolerance allows us to find distraction and emotional distance from difficult emotional situations. ACCEPTS is about distracting yourself until you are ready to deal with a difficult situation or experience. ACCEPTS is an acronym that makes it easier for you to remember to accept the situation for what it is, even if it means stepping away from the situation.

Instead of focusing your energy on changing the situation, focus on ACCEPTS and what it can offer you:

Activities

Engage in any activity that will keep your mind off the negative emotions you are experiencing. If you finish this activity, move on to another. This activity should be healthy, such as listening to music, watching TV, reading, or going for a walk.

Contributions

Do something for someone else. Volunteer your time to help others, donate things you no longer need, make something for someone, or converse with a neighbor.

Comparisons

Find a new perspective. Compare how you feel now to how you felt a few days ago. Compare your life to those less fortunate. The goal of comparisons is to become aware of the perspective you are holding on to and how to change it to be more positive. The intention of this exercise is not to add more pain or distress to your situation.

Emotions

Your mind is powerful, and you can change your current emotion to an opposite emotion. Do an activity that will make you feel a different or opposite emotion from what you currently feel. This will reduce the intensity of your current negative emotion.

Push Away

It is okay to push away the emotionally intense situation _temporarily_. Pushing it away by distracting yourself can give you the time and space you need to be better prepared to take on the situation.

Sensations

Engage your five senses to self-soothe during this challenging time. This can be anything that appeals to your senses, such as music, watching TV, reading, taking a bath or shower, sitting in the sun, or taking a walk in the snow or rain.

Worksheet for Teens: ACCEPTS

In this activity, you will create a list of the things you'll do to distract yourself when facing an unpleasant and challenging situation. Taking a look at the ACCEPTS acronym above, answer the following questions by writing them down for future reference:

- What do you think would be easiest to do?

- What would you prefer to do?

- What type of distraction will you pick for each of the letters?

- What movie, music playlist, or book will you pick?

- What types of puzzles can you do to distract yourself?

- Which of your five senses will soothe you the best?

Focus on creating a thorough list, and place this list on your wall or phone to return to when you need to distract yourself.

Willingness versus Willfulness

Willfulness is when you are determined to do what you want and give no care for the impact it will have on others. In contrast, willingness is being ready to do what is necessary or needed in a given situation. Now, in terms of DBT, willingness is about doing what is effective, using your Wise Mind, becoming aware of how the situation is connected to yourself and others, listening to what the situation is trying to tell you, and asking yourself whether this situation will matter five years from now. Willfulness is stubbornness: it is sitting on your hands when you should be taking action. It's the desire to be right. It's fighting against any suggestions that will improve the situation. It's about being inflexible and rigid. It's about refusing to tolerate the painful moment.

Therefore, your goal will be to practice willingness when you face a distressing situation.

Worksheet for Teens: Willing or Willful?

This exercise will help you solve a problematic situation by teaching you how to evaluate it thoroughly before acting out a solution. When you can solve problematic situations effectively, you are learning to soothe the extreme emotions that arise when faced with emotionally distressing scenarios.

This exercise can be done alone. However, you can ask a parent or teacher to guide you through this activity by helping you look at the situation objectively.

Step 1: Describe It

Describe the problem you are facing. Write down all the facts about the problem: What happened? When did it happen? Who is part of it? Write every factual aspect of the problem down. Do not write your thoughts or feelings down. This step will help you start seeing the situation in a way that will allow you to approach it with willingness, and then come to a solution.

Step 2: How Are You Willful?

In this step, you are going to describe your thoughts and feelings. Reflect on how you resist the situation and the aspects you struggle to tolerate. Once you have this written down, write the possible outcome if you would react to these thoughts and feelings. Then, write down what it is you actually *need* to do to resolve this situation.

Step 3: What Are You Willing to Do?

Explore the alternative to Step 2: What would you feel if you were to accept all the different aspects of this situation? What thoughts will you have? How will you be willing to accept the situation? How will you be willing to do what needs to be done? What would the outcome be if you were to be more flexible, to put your energy towards being willing in the situation?

Take your time and *really* think about this. Ask for guidance from a parent/teacher if you need help to see the situation clearly and find all the facts. Don't rush yourself—rushing through this exercise can lead to doing what you want compared to doing what is needed.

Radical Acceptance

Radical acceptance encourages you to practice using your Wise Mind and accept the moment for what it is. Similarly to willingness, when you can radically accept that the current situation is outside of what you can control, and can do so non-judgmentally, you reduce the suffering this situation can or will cause you.

Radical acceptance is based on the notion that the suffering you experience from difficult situations does not come from the pain of the situation but from your attachment to that pain. In other words, your pain is because you're holding onto what the situation is causing you to feel rather than accepting it and letting go.

When you radically accept a situation, you aim to do this without becoming attached. Detachment does not refer to not feeling your emotions; its goal is actually to help you overcome the situation by not allowing the pain you feel in the situation to turn to suffering.

Radical Acceptance versus Forgiveness

At this point, you might think that no longer being attached to the situation means forgiving it for the pain it has caused you. Many think radical acceptance and forgiveness are the same, but they are not; they are very different. When you practice forgiveness, you are showing kindness to the other person, whereas radical acceptance is showing kindness to yourself.

Are you familiar with the TV show *Avatar: The Last Airbender*? In an episode titled *The Southern Raiders* (Dos Santos, 2008), a character named Katara has the opportunity to face the soldier who killed her mother. The pain of losing her mother caused Katara to act out and be rash in her decisions throughout the show. Katara also believes that killing the man who killed her mother will bring her closure. But when she faces the soldier, she doesn't kill him. Instead, she radically accepts the situation, which helps her let go of the pain and move on. She realizes that killing another will not change anything; it will only make her feelings worse.

Thus, practicing radical acceptance can help you let go of situations or experiences that are causing you to suffer and move beyond them to enjoy life to its fullest by letting go of what is causing you pain.

Worksheet for Teens: Radical Acceptance Statements

In this activity, you will read through the radical acceptance statements and pick your favorite three. Write them down and stick them to your bathroom mirror, ceiling, or any other surface you often look at. Allow these statements to be powerful reminders to accept situations and heal from what is hurting you.

Radical Acceptance Statements (Ayeni, 2023; DBT 2018):

- This is how it has to be.

- The present is the only moment I have control over.

- I can't change what has already happened.

- I can survive this present moment, even if I don't like what is happening.

- I can't control the past.

- This moment is built up of thousands of other decisions.

- Fighting my emotions and thoughts only gives them more power.

- I accept this moment for what it is.

- My emotions are uncomfortable right now, but I'll get through this moment.

- Fighting the past is not helpful.

These distress tolerance skills are not the only skills that are available to you when learning to tolerate distressing situations. In fact, seven other major skills form part of distress tolerance as well. We will be discussing these skills in the next chapter.

Chapter 8: 7 Skills and Techniques

Radical Acceptance is the willingness to experience ourselves and our lives as it is. —
Tara Brach

This chapter aims to provide exercises or activities that teach you distress tolerance. You will note that we cover ACCEPTS and Radical Acceptance again in this chapter. However, our focus is on a different activity relating to these skills. Take your time when working through this chapter, and don't rush through the activities; instead, focus on what you can learn and gain from these skills by taking them slow.

ACCEPTS

Consider this an opportunity to work on your ACCEPTS list and learn the benefits of practicing ACCEPTS when you need to find calm in a difficult situation or problem.

ACCEPTS focuses on doing activities to distract yourself. One of those acts are contributions. In this activity, we will focus on how you can incorporate contributions into your ACCEPTS activities to create a life based on the values you find important and the feeling of overall fulfillment they will provide you.

Worksheet for Teens: Contributions

This activity is based on identifying the aspects of your life that you value the most and focusing on these aspects when faced with a difficult situation. During this activity, you will write down these aspects, why you value them, and how you can build upon them.

If you struggle to choose just three or to determine which aspects you value the most, use a scale of 1 -10 and write down how important you would rate each aspect. This can help you become aware of what you value the most.

Step 1: What You Value the Most

There are certainly aspects of your life that you value more than others, and for everyone, this is different. Some of us value our careers more than our health or value family over work. From the list below, identify three life aspects that you find are most important to you:

- Community

- Educational Goals

- Family

- Friendships

- Health

- Home Life

- Personal Growth

- Recreation and Fun

- Romantic Relationships

- Spirituality and Beliefs

- Work

Step 2: Why They Are Important

List all the reasons why you chose these three values and why they are important to you. Think about how they make you feel and bring meaning into your life. Take your time as you consider every possible reason and write them down.

Step 3: Action for These Values

Consider what activities you can do to incorporate these values into your life more. What activities do you want to do when thinking about these values? Be as specific and realistic about these activities as you can be. Think about how or when you will be doing them, and especially *why* you want to do these activities, and write it all down.

Add these activities to your other ACCEPTS list and use these and the other activities you have listed to help you survive emotionally overwhelming situations that cause you distress.

RESISTT

This technique is all about resisting the urge to act on behaviors that are negative or harmful to you. When you are experiencing overwhelmingly intense emotions that cause you to feel like there is no way out or that the pain will last and never leave you, using RESISTT can help you fight off those urges and focus on more productive and healthy behaviors that instinctively calm you.

Read through each technique carefully, and consider which of the seven techniques you find appealing or willing to try. You can write down the technique you prefer and the activity or action you feel is appropriate.

Worksheet for Teens: RESISTT

Reframe the Situation

When we experience intense and overwhelming emotions, we start thinking a thundercloud will follow us for the rest of our lives. We struggle to see the situation as a single event and start thinking, "Things will never get better" or "My life is terrible". Reframing the situation can help you let go of these negative perspectives and find the silver lining that makes the situation less doom and gloom. Try to see the part of the situation that makes it less horrible.

Engage in a Distracting Activity

Pick an activity that you can engage in to distract you from the intense emotions you are experiencing. Consider the list of activities that you've already written down during your ACCEPTS exercise.

Someone Else

When we get caught up in the storm of our intense emotions, we can find relief from paying attention to someone else. This can come in different forms, such as surprising a friend or a loved one, volunteering, helping a friend or neighbor with an activity, or simply just listening to what someone else has to say.

Intense Sensations

When our emotions are running too high, we can lessen their intensity by giving our mind an intense sensation to focus on instead. Consider the following ways to cause intense but safe sensations: sitting out in the sun, taking a walk in the cold weather, taking a hot or cold shower, or holding an ice cube tightly in your hand.

Shut It Out

When the situation becomes too overwhelming for you, step away from it. If the situation is in a specific place, go to another place if possible. When we can change our environment to one that calms us, we can shut out the distressing situation temporarily until we are more in control of our emotions and thoughts. You can also shut it out by visualizing yourself putting the situation inside a box and then literally setting it aside.

Think Neutral Thoughts

Intense emotions can cause obsessive thoughts to fill our minds and make it difficult not to obsess about a situation. Turning your thoughts away from the situation itself and towards neutral thoughts will allow you to let go of the thought. You can practice neutral thoughts by counting to ten, listing off the colors around you, singing the lyrics to your favorite song, or saying the alphabet backward.

Take a Break

Life goes on even when we are facing an overwhelmingly difficult situation. We have certain responsibilities and chores that we are expected to do in our life. When struggling with these intense emotions, maybe put off a chore or activity for another day (if it's inconsequential) or take a day off of school to have a break from life and stimuli. Avoid taking advantage of this technique by engaging in it too often, but feel confident in using it when you really feel the need.

TIPP

The TIPP technique is about changing your body's chemistry to reduce the physical sensations your overwhelming emotions are causing inside your body. TIPP is effective when you're stuck inside your emotional mind and struggling to control your impulsive behaviors. Using TIPP can help you center yourself and engage your Wise Mind.

Combined Worksheet

For the first time you practice these techniques, it's recommended that you have a parent/teacher present to guide you through each stage of the exercise and ensure that you are doing it properly and effectively. Once you know how to do the exercise, you can do it alone.

__Note:__ If you have any blood pressure or heart problems, an eating disorder, are taking medications such as beta-blockers, or are allergic to cold, please consult your healthcare practitioner before attempting the techniques discussed below.

<u>T</u>emperature

Changing your body's temperature can decrease or increase your heart rate, reducing the intensity of your emotions. If you're feeling 'hot' emotions such as anger, irritation, or rage, change your temperature to something cold. For example, take a cold shower, dip your face into cold water, press an ice pack over your cheeks and eyes, or run an ice cube over your face.

If you're feeling 'cold' emotions such as sadness, anxiety, or depression, turn up your body's temperature. For example, take a hot shower or bath, wrap yourself up in a blanket, or drink a warm beverage.

Intense Exercise

When a situation causes intense emotions, we have a lot of unused energy pent up. Spending this energy can help decrease the intensity of the emotions as we physically and emotionally tire ourselves out. Go for a run, walk around the block as fast as you can, play basketball, dance, lift weights, or do jumping jacks. Try to do this exercise for 10 to 20 minutes, but do not overdo it.

Paced Breathing

Intense emotions bring rise to physical sensations in our bodies. Controlling your breathing can lessen these physical sensations that are building up. Start by breathing deeply in through your nose for five to six seconds, then breathe out through your mouth for a count of seven seconds. Do this for one to two minutes.

Paired Muscle Relaxation

Intense emotions build up in our muscles, causing them to tense up whether we are aware of them or not. In this exercise, you will tense your muscles—which might seem counterproductive, but keep reading—and then relax them. Starting at your toes, work your way up, tense a group of muscles, and then relax them until you reach your face. Tensing these muscles before relaxing them brings your mind's focus to areas where you didn't know tension was building up.

Self-Soothing

As the name suggests, self-soothing is about soothing yourself using your senses. This practice focuses on doing the things you find comforting and enjoyable to reduce feelings of stress, pain, and anxiety.

Below we will list a few things you can do to soothe yourself with your senses. Pick two to three from each list and write them down as a quick toolkit when you need some comfort. If there is an activity you would prefer doing that's not listed here, write it down for yourself. We are all different and find different things soothing.

Worksheet for Teens

Read the lists below and pick two to three activities that you like or think will be most effective in giving you comfort.

Sight:

- Take a walk in nature or a park and observe everything around you.

- Look at images of things you find soothing.

- Watch videos that make you laugh or feel happy.

- Go to a museum or take a virtual tour of one.

- Watch a movie that's comforting and has a happy ending.

Hearing:

- Listen to classical or instrumental music.

- Listen to music you find enjoyable.

- Sit in a park and listen to all the sounds around you.

- Take a walk around your neighborhood and listen to what you can hear.

- Listen to a podcast or audiobook.

- Listen to the sounds of the ocean, forests, or rain.

Smell:

- Light a fragrant candle.

- Light incense.

- Put a few drops of lavender in a humidifier.

- Wear your favorite fragrance.

- Go to places that appeal to your sense of smell, for example, a restaurant, bakery, or perfume store.

Taste:

- Eat your favorite food, savoring every bite.

- Eat some snacks or comfort foods.

- Make yourself a warm beverage.

- Eat fresh fruits.

- Eat some sweets.

Touch:

- Wear comfortable clothes.

- Cuddle with your pet.

- Wrap yourself in a blanket.

- Take a bubble bath.

- Play with play-dough or a sensory toy.

- Moisturize your skin.

Grounding

Grounding refers to reconnecting yourself to the present moment. When you experience intense emotions, you can drift away from the present and start to revisit the past or think about the future, similar to a balloon that's not kept in place. Grounding yourself allows you to deal with your emotions rather than run away from them.

Worksheet for Teens

This exercise aims to bring you back to the here and now. The key to using grounding tools is to recognize when you are drifting away from the present moment because it is too painful or trying to avoid the current situation. This exercise incorporates elements of mindfulness that we've already covered.

Step 1: Describe

Duration: 10 minutes.

Have a look at where you are and what you can observe about your environment. Start describing what you see: What colors, shapes, sizes, and textures do you are present around you? Focus on each object long enough to notice what it looks like and then move to the next.

Step 2: Breathe

Duration: 5 minutes.

Once you are done observing your environment, focus on your breathing. Start breathing deeply into your stomach and then slowly settle into a normal breathing rhythm.

Step 3: Become Mindful

Duration: 5 minutes.

Notice the physical sensations of your body as you sit or stand in this environment. What can you feel? Are you comfortable? Are you tired? Do you feel tense? Can you feel your feet on the ground? Do your arms feel heavy?

Step 4: Observe With More

Duration: 5 minutes.

Engage all your other senses: Do you hear a loud sound? Can you feel your clothes against your skin? What do you smell? Be open to whatever you are experiencing with your senses.

This exercise will help you become immediately aware of your environment and works well in a crisis compared to mindfulness skills that practice your Wise Mind muscle. It is effective because it works at immediately bringing your focus to the here and now, compared to participating in an exercise that's done outside of a crisis.

Pros and Cons

Creating a cost-benefit analysis, a pros and cons list, can help you make better and more informed decisions. It also helps you recognize problematic behavior and work towards changing this behavior to those that will serve you better.

We don't always recognize our problematic behavior or look at the damage it will do in the long-run. Yes, in the current moment, this behavior brings instant relief from intense emotions, but it's not allowing us to be mindful and tolerant of what we are experiencing.

Worksheet for Teens

Weighing the pros and cons of your behavior will take time—a lot of time—but once you have repeated this exercise three or more times, you will recognize problematic behavior easier and be able to work towards engaging in behavior that will serve you in the long-run.

Get a piece of paper and a pen and recreate the table below on it.

Old Behavior:	
Cons:	**Pros:**
• • • • • •	• • • • • •
Total score:	Total score:
Changed Behavior:	
Cons:	**Pros:**
• • • • • •	• • • • • •
Total score:	Total score:

Step 1: Choose a Behavior

Take a moment to think about behaviors that aren't benefiting you. They can be anything. Think about possible habits that you want to change. Maybe you already tried changing them, but it didn't work. These can be behaviors such as spending too much money, spending too much time playing games or being on your phone, or eating too much. Really think about these habits that you want to change. Now pick one and write it down in the given space.

Step 2: Cons of this Behavior

Write down every negative consequence or aspect of this behavior and what it causes. Allow yourself the time to brainstorm these cons. Start with the obvious ones that you already know, then dive deeper into the problematic behavior and expand on it. At first, this won't be easy, but it will become easier with practice.

Step 3: Pros of This Behavior

Write down every reason for why you engage in this behavior. We engage in these problematic behaviors because they provide us with immediate benefits that are short-term. These reasons are what made this behavior feel good and why you turned to this behavior when dealing with intense and overwhelming emotions.

Step 4: Cons of Changed Behavior

Now, turn this behavior into one you think will serve you better. Changing a habit or behavior takes a lot of time and energy and requires you to move outside of what is comfortable for you. Write down the alternative to your problematic behavior, and in the space provided, list all the cons of making this change.

Step 5: Pros of Changed Behavior

After listing all the cons, focus on the possible benefits of this changed behavior. Be creative and have fun with this. These pros can be anything. Start with how changing one habit or behavior will slowly improve small things in your life, then look at the benefits of this behavior in the long run. Write it all down.

Step 6: Score These Cons and Pros

Think of yourself as a teacher and score each of your pros and cons from one to five (five being the most important) on how important these reasons are to you. As you continue to score these benefits and consequences of your behavior, you'll come to realize that what you thought was important about your problematic behavior might not be.

Now compare the points of importance of your problematic behavior against your changed behavior. You will notice that your problematic behavior is costing you more than the changed behavior and that the changed behavior is more beneficial to you.

Keep this piece of paper close to you for when you feel the urge to engage in your problematic behavior to remind yourself of the cost and benefits of that behavior compared to the alternative behavior you've decided on practicing.

Radical Acceptance

Have you picked out three statements from the previous chapter to carry with you or keep somewhere you can be reminded of them? When we experience intense negative emotions, our actions towards these emotions are often negative. This is often because we haven't accepted past events and are still experiencing the need to change what has already happened. So when we encounter similar events, we cling to our previous reactions.

Worksheet for Teens: Bonus Activity

To change our reactions to negative emotions, we need to release our death grip on past events that fuel these negative reactions. This is the only way that we can change something about a problematic situation. Releasing our death grip on these events is about accepting the past event and recognizing that our energy shouldn't be focused on holding on but on letting go.

Follow these steps to accept these events and take control of your reactions and behaviors.

Step 1: An Important Event

Start by thinking about a past event that is important to you but that you are having a hard time accepting. It can be something more current or something from your past that you often obsess over or regret when thinking of the event.

Step 2: What Caused It

Think about all the facts that led up to this event. Then, consider all the facts that make this event hard to accept. Try to stay away from judgmental statements or turn the blame on yourself. State only the facts and don't judge them as good or bad. This doesn't undermine the pain of the event but allows you to see the bigger picture of the event.

Step 3: Accept What You Feel

What do you feel when thinking about this event? What other emotions come to the surface? Be honest and take your time as you observe every sensation of the event. Were your palms sweaty? Did you feel anger, frustration, or shame? Think about this emotion and accept it fully. Remember, you can't change what has already happened, but you can change how you react to what has happened. Accepting all you feel allows you to ease some of your grip on this event.

Step 4: Be Proactive

This step is about making a proactive plan about the situation or its effects on you. If this event doesn't have a major impact on you, then you only need the above steps, but if this event has a firmer grip on you, you will need to come up with how you will improve this situation by using the Wise Mind exercise from the previous chapters. Use your wise mind to look at possible solutions or experiences that are hidden deeper and require your acceptance of them.

Throughout this chapter, we have looked at ways in which you can master techniques to help you tolerate distressing situations. With the seven techniques listed above, you might not have a manual on how to survive life's challenging moments, but you now have a survival guide filled with the techniques and knowledge you have gained from Distress

Tolerance, and this will guide you in handling difficult situations with mindfulness, understanding, and acceptance—even when acceptance isn't always easy.

Part 4: Emotion Regulation

Chapter 9: Myths About Emotions

According to a study commissioned by Movember, seventy-seven percent of men believe that talking about their feelings helps them deal with these emotions. Yet, fifty-eight percent feel that society expects them to be strong and show no weakness when it comes to their emotions. —Ipsos MORI & Movember

There exist various theories about emotions: Some suggest there are only six primary emotions; others believe that our physical reactions cause our emotions instead of the other way around; or, they believe that emotions and reactions happen simultaneously and one doesn't influence the other.

Our focus here is on the emotions we experience and how they trigger physical and behavioral reactions. We will examine the six basic emotions that everyone is born with, how triggers shape emotions, what emotions are *not*, and the misconceptions surrounding them. Lastly, we will explore emotional regulation and how it can help combat feelings of anxiety, nervousness, inadequacy, worry, and fear.

What Emotions Are

Consider the range of emotions you've experienced recently: Can you identify them all? Were some of them enjoyable? If you had to explain these emotions to a robot that has no knowledge of them and will never experience them, would you describe them in a positive or negative light? It's not a simple task, is it? The question "What are emotions?" can be difficult to answer, as many of us have a limited understanding of their origins, triggers, and internal effects.

What Are Emotions?

Emotions result from changes in your mind's functioning that give rise to conscious mental reactions to these changes. Simply put, emotions come from your mind as a response to an event that has changed the functioning of your mind.

Some emotions we experience in certain situations are due to automatic reactions in our mind. For instance, if you experienced an event where people loudly screamed at each other, you might become triggered when hearing someone yell, being yelled at, or seeing someone being yelled at, even a long time after the initial event. Triggers are reminders or experiences that cause you to feel certain emotions connected to another event and relive them.

Triggers and emotions have a complex relationship. An event can trigger emotions, but a trigger can also cause an emotion. Triggers aren't always negative, nor are emotions. Some triggers can bring comfort or happiness, while others can bring anger, rage, or sadness. By controlling our reactions to our emotions, we can examine what has triggered us and change our automatic responses to regulate our emotions and behaviors.

Emotions are not limited to our minds; they are also felt in our bodies and behavior. Therefore, emotions have three elements that contribute to our experience of them: firstly, emotions are subjective, as the anger we feel when hurt is different from the anger we feel when scared; secondly, emotions are accompanied by physical sensations, such as a clenched stomach when anxious or a racing heart when angry; lastly, emotions are reflected in our behavior. For instance, when we are happy, we may talk more, dance, or invite others to join in our joy. Conversely, when we are sad, we may withdraw from others or listen to loud music.

Our emotions cause a reaction throughout our entire body and mind. It isn't just something we feel in our minds but in our bodies and actions as well.

Primary Emotions

We have six primary emotions that we are born with: happiness, sadness, fear, anger, surprise, and disgust. When you experience different intensities of these emotions or a combination of them, you are experiencing something different from those listed here, but still, at their core, they are part of these primary emotions. For example, experiencing different fear levels can make you feel anxious, powerless, or overwhelmed. Experiencing fear and sadness can cause you to feel despair.

Think of these six primary emotions as primary colors. You are a painter, and as you experience different events throughout your life, you mix different colors together to make a new color (emotion) that you can experience. Think about an emotion as part of the primary six, the colors that created this emotion. Is it a combination of colors or a single color experienced more intensely?

Now that we know what emotions are, let's look at common myths and misconceptions about them.

What Emotions Are Not

Our emotions are confusing, complicated, overwhelming, and sometimes downright scary. And sometimes, we fight against our emotions or struggle with them. Before I tell you why you're possibly fighting with your emotions, look at the list below. Are you noticing if you are:

- suppressing your emotions by pushing them away or bottling them up?

- distracting yourself from your emotions?

- numbing yourself to your emotions?

- avoiding places, people, or experiences because of the emotions they cause?

- punishing yourself for feeling a certain way?

- letting your emotions highjack your decisions, behavior, and life?

If you relate to any of these, you might be holding onto misconceptions and myths about emotions, and you're trying to behave according to these misconceptions while consequently causing yourself unnecessary suffering. When we hold onto misconceptions or myths about emotions, we are causing our emotions to impact our experiences, relationships, and lives negatively. Letting go of these misconceptions, we start to live with meaning, become adaptive to our situations, and forge an alliance with our emotional mind rather than being in a constant battle with it—a battle neither will win.

Below we will provide you with a list of misconceptions and myths. Take a moment to read each of one carefully and think about it. Ask yourself whether you believe this myth.

Take note of that myth and move to the next one, repeating the process. Once you've read them carefully, answer these questions: Which myths did you believe were true? Which did you know were false?

Myths and Misconceptions

Myth 1: Emotions Make Us Illogical and Irrational

This myth stems from the idea that your rational mind and your emotional mind stand in opposition to each other, constantly at war. As you've come to realize, though these two parts of your mind can exist together within your Wise Mind.

Myth 2: Expressing Emotions is a Sign of Weakness

This is one of the most damaging misconceptions because it encourages us to deny a vital part of who we are. In truth, expressing your emotions takes courage, and the strength to face the emotions you are feeling and to express them in a healthy way.

Myth 3: Some Emotions are Bad

"Good Vibes Only!" We've seen this statement everywhere, and many of the people we watch on social media try to live by these words. The truth is, it's impossible. You cannot deny one part of your experiences and accept the other part. Think of an everyday object. Now cut it in half. Is it still functional? Can you still use it, or does it need its other half to make sense? The same goes for you. You need all of you to experience life, which includes emotions that aren't always pleasant.

Myth 4: Emotions Can't Be Controlled

This is one of the most common misconceptions surrounding emotions. Our emotions can surprise or overwhelm us, but we aren't prisoners to our emotions. The truth is when our emotions feel too powerful, it is often because we have forgotten that we are powerful too. Now, we can't drop-kick those emotions, but we can lessen the power they hold over us and take back some control.

Myth 5: All Emotions Must Be Expressed

Not everything you feel should be expressed. You don't leave the bathroom and give your friends a play-by-play about what you did inside it. No, and the same goes for your emotions. Sometimes we feel the urge to express what we are feeling and to get it off our chest, but before we do this, we should consider whether expressing this emotion is effective, because we risk fuelling that emotion by expressing it. For example, punching a wall when angry will likely only increase your anger.

Myth 6: Strong Emotions Mean You're Out of Control

Intense and extreme emotions can feel out of control because of our reactions. Therefore, it's not your emotions that cause you to be out of control but rather your reaction to these emotions. When you leave your reactions unchecked, you risk reacting to urges that cause you to feel out of control.

Myth 7: Emotions Speak the Truth

This way of thinking is a trap! Your emotions are not based on the facts of the experience. Your emotions are based on your *interpretation* of the experience. Your emotions are not 'speaking' some absolute truth; they are the reactions you have to a situation and the perspective you have on the situation.

Myth 8: I Am My Emotions

You're not an animated character with a rain cloud following you around when you're sad or smoke blowing out your ears when you're angry—even if your anger can feel like that sometimes. You are more than the emotions you feel. Your emotions are only a part of who you are. You're not a sad person because you feel sad; this simply means you're experiencing something sad, but you remain who you are regardless of your emotions.

None of these statements are true. We have misconceptions about our emotions because of the falsehoods people devised about emotions when they didn't know better. We provided the above myths and their truths to show you that these myths are constant only because people spread the misinformation in ads, social media, books, TV shows, movies, and so forth, whether intentionally or not. If you become aware of these misconceptions, you can learn from them and find peace in your Wise Mind.

Emotional Regulation: What Does It Look Like?

Emotional regulation is the ability to control your emotions by recognizing, managing, and responding to your emotions in an adaptive and healthy way that allows you to feel calm and in control even when experiencing these extreme emotions. Emotional regulation includes naming and understanding your emotions, decreasing the frequency at which you experience negative emotions, and decreasing your vulnerability to overwhelming and extreme emotions, and to the anxieties and stresses that cause you pain.

Regulating your emotions gives you control over how you react to your emotions instead of feeling out of control. Practicing emotional regulation can allow you to think clearly, allowing you to make decisions and choices that are intentional rather than mere impulsive responses to emotions. Your relationships with others will also improve as you can listen when others are talking to you and communicate your needs instead of growing angry or irritated with friends and family. Most of all, when you gain control over extreme and overwhelming emotions, you can lessen the intensity of these emotions and lessen your overall feelings of anxiety, stress, fear, and worry.

Now that you have a better idea of what emotional regulation is and its benefits for you, we are ready to move on to the next chapter, where you will learn how to practice it.

Chapter 10: Skills and Techniques

Emotion can be the enemy, if you give into your emotion, you lose yourself. You must be at one with your emotions, because the body always follows the mind. —Bruce Lee

In this chapter, we discuss five emotion regulation skills and techniques you can practice and work through. These skills and techniques will help you find ways to take back control of your ability to control your emotions and, in doing so, will lessen some of the unnecessary anxieties and stress you are experiencing.

STOP

The STOP skill is one of the crisis survival skills. It's been adapted for almost every crisis you might face. In DBT, STOP is used as an "emergency mindfulness" skill, when your emotions threaten to get the best of you and push you towards unhelpful actions.

Worksheet for Teens

This skill is best practiced before attempting to use it when emotions are running high. Use this skill when you feel that the current moment is becoming a bigger problem or when you anticipate that your emotions will intensify and become overwhelming.

Step 1: <u>S</u>top

If you feel your emotions are running high and out of control, stop. Freeze in the moment, and don't react. Don't do or say anything. Simply stop, take a deep breath, and focus on the emotion or emotions you are feeling. Put a name to that emotion.

Step 2: _Take a Step Back_

When emotions are running high, and the situation is charged, it isn't easy to deal with it all on the spot. This step encourages you to take a temporary break from the situation. During this moment of stepping back, focus on breathing deeply until you feel in control again.

Step 3: _Observe_

As you breathe, observe your surroundings. What is happening? Who is involved? What are other people saying or doing? Notice the negative thoughts you have about the situation. What are the facts? Remember to avoid jumping to conclusions; instead, calmly and slowly look at all the facts and the various options available to you.

Step 4: _Proceed Mindfully_

Now that you have become aware of the situation and all the facts, answer these questions: What do you want from this situation? What are your goals? What choice will make this situation better? What choice will make this situation worse? Remain calm and stay in control as you answer these questions. After gathering all the information, you will be better prepared to deal with this situation. Remember, your mind needs time to think things through. Then proceed to resolve the situation effectively.

ABC PLEASE

ABC PLEASE is a skill set focused on helping you build up positive emotions and experiences, decrease negative emotions, and learn the importance of self-care that leads to more confidence and joy and builds resilience. These skills will help to reduce feelings of vulnerability, such as hopelessness or helplessness, and allow you to be prepared when faced with an emotional crisis.

Part 1: ABC

Skill 1: Accumulate Positive Experiences

As life gets busy, we often forget to do what we enjoy. And when we've had a rough week where things just keep piling up, we forget to do what makes us happy, instead obsessing over everything that is wrong and that could go wrong. This skill focuses on taking the necessary steps to do what you enjoy regularly.

Skill 2: Build Mastery

This skill focuses on learning and then mastering a new skill. When we master a new skill or succeed in doing something new, it fills us with confidence and reduces vulnerable emotions. Building mastery teaches us to assume that we will succeed at any task we face, compared to thinking we will fail because we feel vulnerable. This is a skill that we will focus on later in this chapter.

Skill 3: Cope Ahead

Cope ahead focuses on being prepared for the situation. If you know an upcoming event will be challenging, take the time to prepare for it mentally and emotionally. We'll look more at how to cope ahead later in this chapter.

Part 2: PLEASE

Skill 1: Physical Illness

When you are sick, you feel miserable and dread any task or activity you need to do. Ignoring your needs when you are sick will only intensify your misery and dread. This step is about knowing when your body needs to be cared for. You cannot perform your best when sick, which impacts your emotions. Get well again first. Everything else can wait.

Skill 2: Eating

Having balanced meals daily allows your body to perform optimally while ensuring you have the energy you need to make it through the day. Living off of caffeine will only cause you to crash later in the day. Instead, eat balanced meals that give you steady energy throughout the day. When you're hungry or your body lacks nutrients, your mind becomes clouded and emotions can run rampant. Try to lower your caffeine intake and eat balanced meals. Don't skip meals, but try to eat every meal, even if it's just a few bites.

Skill 3: Avoid Mood-Altering Substances

This doesn't refer to prescribed medications you should be taking. Some teenagers and adults rely on substances to cope with difficult situations, but these substances often alter our moods further. If you're drinking alcohol, misusing prescription medications or other substances, know that these affect your emotions more than you realize, and you will benefit more from avoiding these substances than using them.

Skill 4: Sleep

Growing up, we all thought sleeping as little as possible was great. We might have even bragged about not sleeping all night because we were doing something else. But the problem with this is that your body needs you to get adequate and restful sleep to bring balance to your mind and body. When you sleep, your body can regulate itself, while your mind regulates your emotions. Balanced sleep reduces feelings of tiredness, exhaustion, irritability, and anxiety.

Skill 5: Exercise

This is a skill many of us neglect, but physical exercise is vital to our physical, mental, and emotional health. When we engage in physical activity, we lessen the intensity of our emotions, decrease negative emotions, and work out some of the pent-up energy caused by these intense emotions. Over time this skill will build up our resilience to intense emotions.

Now this doesn't mean you have to go at this skill so hard that you're soaked with sweat. No, it is about doing any physical activity for at least 20 minutes a day. This can be walking in the park or around your neighborhood, swimming, dancing, or playing a sport—anything that gets your body moving.

Cope Ahead

As mentioned earlier, coping ahead is about preparing yourself in some way for an event or situation and reducing stress ahead of time. We all had to get up in front of the class and deliver a presentation. Before this presentation, we prepared, researched, and wrote down some notes for ourselves. Doing this increased our chances of getting a good grade, but it also taught us the benefit of being prepared beforehand.

Worksheet for Teens

You will need a paper and a pen for this exercise.

Step 1: Describe the Situation

Think about a situation that is likely to cause you to feel uncomfortable emotions. Once you have a situation in mind, start writing down all the facts about this situation. Be specific. Name the emotions likely to come to the surface in this situation and those that will interfere with you using your skills.

Step 2: Decide On a Skill

During this book, you've learned valuable skills that can help you in the situation you described above. Think about what skill will be best suited for this situation. Be specific and write down all the details of how you will cope ahead with this situation using this specific skill. Also, write down how the skill will help you with your emotions and reactions.

Step 3: Imagine the Situation

With all the details written down, imagine this situation as vividly as possible. Be sure to imagine yourself in the situation and not outside looking in.

Step 4: Rehearse

Now that you're imagining this situation vividly, rehearse how you will effectively cope during this situation. Rehearse how you will put the skill to use. Rehearse the emotions you will feel, the thoughts you will have, and the words you will say. Rehearse *how* you will say these words. Rehearse what you will do if the situation intensifies—how will you calm it back down? Rehearse all the worst-case scenarios, so you know exactly how you will feel and can go about coping with the situation.

Step 5: Relax

Rehearsing a situation can often leave us tense. Use one of the techniques for relaxation that you enjoyed here to calm yourself down.

Positive Self-Talk

Sometimes all we have is self-talk to push us through difficult situations. Consider the stories of those who have survived terrible situations, from being lost in the desert to being lost at sea, and how these people believed they couldn't carry on anymore but then survived. Want to know their secret? They turned their negative self-talk into positive self-talk, and by doing so, they filled themselves with the power and energy to carry on and not give up.

We all have negative things we say about ourselves. These are often a result of what others have said to us or of our experiences. And these negative self-talks are powerful because when we repeat things over and over again, we give them power over us. Over time, these talks become our truths. To turn this process around, repeating positive self-talk affirmations over and over again will give them the power instead.

Worksheet for Teens

Positive self-talk might be the life raft you need during a dire situation. Never forget that your words are powerful. Therefore, read over the provided list of affirmations and pick five of your favorite affirmations. Write them down and place them where you will see them daily. At first, you won't believe in these affirmations, but they will become your truth over time.

Affirmations:

- I AM BEAUTIFUL, CONFIDENT, AND INTELLIGENT.
- I LIKE MYSELF.
- I AM A WARRIOR.
- I AM LOVED.
- I HAVE DONE A LOT TO BE PROUD OF.
- I HAVE FRIENDS AND FAMILY WHO CARE ABOUT ME.
- I AM HANDSOME.
- I AM IN CONTROL.
- I AM PERFECTLY IMPERFECT.
- I AM THE BEST ME.
- MY LIFE HAS PURPOSE.
- THERE IS NO ONE ELSE I WOULD RATHER BE.
- I AM BLESSED.
- TODAY IS MY DAY.
- I WILL DANCE IN THE RAIN.
- MY LIFE HAS HOPE.
- MY SOUL SINGS.
- I AM CAPABLE OF WISE CHOICES.
- EVERY MOMENT IS BEAUTIFUL IN ITS OWN WAY.
- I'LL STOP TO SMELL THE ROSES.
- LIFE IS WORTH EVERY MOMENT.
- I WILL HOLD MY HEAD HIGH.

Build Mastery

You build mastery when you do the things you enjoy and do them well. This process is about making small changes to achieve or accomplish something that makes us feel good about ourselves. Building mastery makes you feel competent, confident, in control, and empowered. It's about training yourself to commit to something and see it through to the end.

DBT asks you to accept what you can't change and change what you can. Building mastery gives you the skills to plan out a change you want to make in your life, such as reaching a goal and then committing to that goal. You're going to be making these small and big changes when adjusting your thinking, how you talk to yourself, and how you behave when feeling intense emotions, and this all requires you to take steps towards change. But change doesn't happen overnight. It doesn't happen in three big steps. It happens in the small achievable steps you take every single day.

Worksheet for Teens

For this exercise, you will need a pen and paper. This exercise may take some time to work through, but as you decide on a skill, it will become easier to lay out the steps you have to take. Remember, this task teaches you to work towards goals and make small improvements over time.

Step 1: Plan For Success

Think about a skill you always wanted to learn or one you've tried already but want to master. As you think about this new skill, be sure that it's something possible and achievable. This will ensure that you set yourself up for success instead of failure.

Write down what this new skill is and all that you want to accomplish with this skill.

Step 2: Small Steps

If you want to create your own game, you won't jump in head first and start writing the game code. You need to start small and set realistic goals, such as learning the coding language first. Then you'll write your first small program, gradually increasing the complexity of the programs you write until you can start shaping the pieces of your gaming code.

Small steps will keep you motivated and committed to the goal you set for yourself. If you're unsure of how to proceed, write down all the steps you can think of to reach this goal and, where needed, research these steps.

Step 3: Do It Everyday

Some days you will make fantastic progress, and others not so much, but as long as you practice your skill every day, even if it's just a little bit, you're already taking the steps towards reaching your end goal. Progress is progress, no matter how small of a step it is.

Set time aside every day for you to work on this skill.

Step 4: Celebrate Each Step

Write down your progress, or create a chart that you can color in to show the progress you have made thus far. Seeing your progress will motivate and excite you about reaching that finish line. As you complete a milestone, celebrate that achievement. Take time to acknowledge all you have done to reach this step and be proud of yourself. What you are doing is hard work, but it will all be worth it.

And when you've reached that finish line, start dreaming about your next goal. Once you've accomplished that goal, you'll be ready for something more challenging and will discover an endless world of possibilities waiting for you. Take small steps to make big leaps in your life!

In the next chapter, we will look at another major skill of emotional regulation that is incredibly helpful to those who use DBT. This skill will be tricky to master at first, but it will be well worth it.

Chapter 11: Opposite Action

Dialectical Behavior Therapy theorizes that changing actions—even when not done genuinely—leads to changed emotions. —Evolve Treatment Center

We've singled out opposite action because this skill requires your full attention to understand how and when to use it, and also when *not* to. Opposite action, as it suggests, is doing the opposite action to something. In terms of DBT, opposite action is choosing to respond opposite to the urges that your emotions activate within you. You would do the opposite of what you feel like doing because, in the present moment, your emotions have overridden your rational mind.

In short, opposite action is about turning your negative or unhealthy responses to emotions into healthier responses that will help improve your control over your emotions, reinforce positive action, and decrease prolonged pain caused by unchecked emotions.

Opposite action is not about ignoring your emotions but about acknowledging them, understanding why you feel them, and not acting on the urges caused by these emotions unless the action is *justified*. Opposite action should be used in situations when your emotions *don't* fit the situation or aren't fully justified. For example, you're walking home in the dark, and two shadowy figures are approaching you from behind. You're going to feel anxious. This emotion fits the situation, and the urge to cross the street or find a safe area is justified. These actions are activated by your mind's fight-or-flight response and rely on both your emotional and rational mind.

If you feel guilty and ashamed because you took money out of your mother's purse without telling her, and she's asking everyone in the house if they took it, those feelings do fit the situation. You will not use opposite action; instead, you'll use your Wise Mind to resolve the situation of your dishonesty. In the previous example, you will not calmly approach the figures walking behind you—that will only put you in further danger.

This is why it's also important to understand when it's appropriate to use opposite action and when it is not. We will provide you with the skills and steps to know whether the situation requires opposite action and how to use the skill.

Opposite Action In Action

Before we jump right into the step-by-step instructions for using opposite action, let's look at in-depth examples to help you visually understand how opposite action works and the benefits it will provide you when it comes to regulating your emotions and lessening unnecessary anxiety and suffering.

Emotion: Fear

Action Urge: Run away or avoid

Opposite Action: Approach or don't avoid

In Action:

Example 1: A teenager who is overweight might fear the judgment of those around them and eat their lunch in the bathroom away from everyone else. However, this fear is *not justified* because no one has bullied this teenager about their weight. The right course of action will be to stop fearing situations that aren't happening and sit among their friends in the cafeteria at lunch. In their opposite action to their emotion, they could regulate their emotion by logically viewing the facts of the situation.

Example 2: A teenager wants to try out for a sport at their new school. They love this sport, but they are afraid of failing, of not making the team. So instead of going to tryouts, they go home, and their anxiety builds up as the time for tryouts is running out. This fear is *not justified*. The right action for them would be to go to the tryouts because they will not know the outcome unless they try. In doing the opposite of what their emotion told them to, they will stop worrying about the future, regulate their emotion, and go to that tryout. They will know they've tried their best, whether they succeed or fail. If they hadn't, they would have obsessively wondered whether they could have made the team if they did go to the tryout.

Worksheet for Teens

Suppose you're in a situation where you feel overpowered by the urges of your emotions. In that case, use the flow diagram to determine whether to focus on opposite action or to move toward problem-solving.

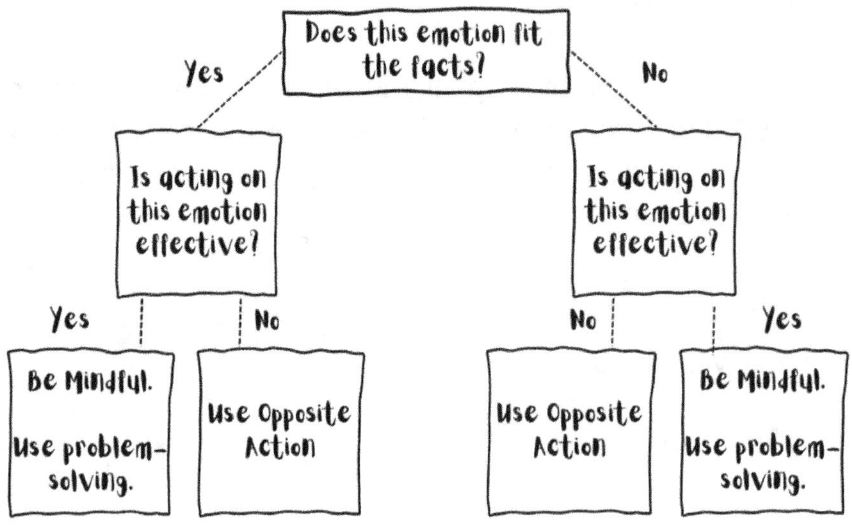

Opposite Action: Step-By-Step

You will need a pen and paper for this exercise.

Step 1: Identify and Name

Think of situations where your emotions cause you to act on certain urges. Identify this emotion and name it, similarly to what we did in the above example. This emotion is often one that you know needs to change because the actions it causes are harmful to you or your relationships.

Step 2: Check the Facts

Now that you know which emotion you are dealing with, think about whether this emotion fits the situation. Is your emotion justified? Does the intensity of this emotion match that of the situation? Does the duration of this emotion fit the situation?

Step 3: Identify and Describe

Think about the urges you feel when experiencing this emotion: What does the emotion make you want to do? Identify the action the emotion causes and describe how you act upon this urge. Write down what acting on this urge does: Who does it affect? How is it harmful or ineffective for you?

Step 4: Ask Your Wise Mind

Sit and think about the situation, the emotion, and the urges. Ask your Wise Mind to help you identify these actions and urges and to help you determine possible effective actions you can take. Write down what comes to mind—it can be anything. This step is to help you think of how to be effective.

Step 5: Do the Opposite

You've written down your action urges and what your Wise Mind has offered as a solution. Now, write an action that's the opposite of your urge. For example, if your action urge is to avoid, the opposite would be not to avoid. If it's to remain in bed, the opposite would be to get out of bed. See whether the opposite action matches the solution your Wise Mind has offered. As you continue doing this exercise, your Wise Mind will intuitively learn when opposite action is the most effective.

Step 6: Do It All The Way

Now that you know what your action should be, act upon that action. Do it fully and all the way. Don't do it halfway or only partly because it will just be ineffective. If it's to get out of bed, get up and out of bed, do not get up and lie on the couch. That's simply changing the location and not changing the urge.

Step 7: Repeat

To make this new action stick, you will need to continue doing the opposite of the urge until it sticks. When your urge changes to the opposite action urge, you have effectively succeeded in changing the urges this emotion causes within you, allowing you to better regulate your emotions and the reactions they cause.

Practice Activity

Think of a recent situation in which your emotions took control of your actions. Apply the above steps to that encounter. Would the situation have turned out differently? Would doing the opposite of what you did have caused more favorable results in that situation? Would opposite action have been inappropriate for that situation?

Do you see how opposite action would have benefitted you in this situation? Is there another situation that you can think of? Apply opposite action to that situation too. The more you practice these situations with opposite actions, the more you develop the skill and teach your mind and yourself that you have control over the actions your emotions cause.

Now that we've reached the end of our practice of Emotional Regulation, are you more aware of how your emotions have impacted your choices, decisions, and actions in life? Can you see how emotions aren't always right or how we believe in myths about our emotions that build upon our anxieties? Remember that your emotions are powerful, but so are you, and you're capable of taking control over the emotions you experience, the actions you take, and the things you do to lessen your pain and suffering. Regulating your emotions takes time—take it step by step, and before you know it, you'll have mastered being effective in your life.

Part 5: Interpersonal Effectiveness

Chapter 12: Boundaries and Barriers

Of course, setting boundaries isn't easy. It's uncomfortable and forces a teen to stand up for themselves and draw some lines in the sand…Yet, it's one of the most important things teens need to learn how to do. —Sherri Gordon

What Is Interpersonal Effectiveness?

Interpersonal effectiveness refers to the skills used to interact with ourselves and others. It's about how we establish and maintain the relationships we have with others by communicating effectively. The aim of interpersonal effectiveness is to strengthen our current relationships, build new relationships, and end relationships that are toxic or unhealthy. It's important that we maintain a balance in our relationships, the same way we maintain balance in the rest of our lives.

The two major aspects of interpersonal effectiveness are asking for the things we need and learning to say no—resisting the pressure to overstep these aspects. Apart from these aspects, when we interact with others, we do this with three goals in mind: the first is objective effectiveness, which focuses on what we want to get out of the relationship; the second goal is relationship/connection effectiveness, which is our goal of improving or maintaining relationships; lastly, self-respect effectiveness focuses on how we maintain and cultivate self-respect in these relationships with others and also within ourselves.

Factors that influence interpersonal effectiveness include worrying thoughts, emotional reactions, indecisions, and other factors that lead to a decrease in how comfortably we interact and communicate with those around us. However, the benefits of interpersonal effectiveness are an increase in effective communication, self-respect, boundaries, building mastery, and balancing our priorities and demands in life.

In short, it's about balancing our wants and shoulds—making sure that we maintain a balance between the things we want to do (pleasurable activities) and what we should do (responsibilities). The relationships around us impact our emotions, how we perceive the world, and the outlook we have on life. By maintaining healthy relationships with others, we are ensuring that our lives are filled with people who improve our experiences and who we can rely on, support, and care about. When our relationships with others are good, we experience less anxiety, we have a support system that can help us through difficult times, and we are no longer suffering due to unhealthy or toxic relationships that cause us unnecessary pain.

The Importance of Boundaries

Boundaries are the limits we set with others to protect ourselves. They're also our expression of self-worth, and they let people know what we value, how we want to be treated, and what we are uncomfortable with. Healthy boundaries are essential to successful relationships, whether platonic or romantic.

When we set physical and emotional boundaries, we are fostering relationships that are respectful, supportive, and healthy. Unfortunately, many of us, teenagers and adults included, have trouble setting boundaries with our friends and romantic partners, and when this happens, we put ourselves at risk of getting hurt, being bullied, or experiencing a relationship that's abusive. That being said, it's not easy setting boundaries, and it can make us uncomfortable since it forces us to stand up for ourselves.

Boundaries are a protective wall we put up to protect us from unwanted physical contact, the feelings, words, ideas, and judgments of others, all while maintaining a relationship with someone. When our boundaries are too open, we run the risk of being unable to protect ourselves, and the thoughts and judgments of others will impact us negatively. When our boundaries are too closed, we risk being shut off from the world and the people around us, we are unable to connect with others, and we will find it difficult to let others come near us for fear of being hurt.

Therefore, it's important that the boundaries we set allow us enough protection to be safe in the relationships we share with others while also ensuring they aren't closing us off from the world around us.

Interpersonal Effectiveness Barriers

While boundaries help us maintain interpersonal effectiveness, barriers can prevent us from being assertive with our boundaries which impacts the relationships we have with others. Below we are going to briefly discuss the five most common barriers to assertiveness. Some of these barriers might be familiar to you already.

Barrier 1: Old Patterns

Our upbringing and relationships with others can have an influence on the way that we communicate in our current relationships. During this time, we have learned habits in the way we communicate that may not be assertive. We might be more passive in our communication, or more aggressive. Defaulting to these old patterns may not be the most effective way for us to communicate and might be the wall standing in the way of what we want.

Passive patterns refer to patterns where you surrender to the conflict by becoming silent or agreeing because you fear possible conflict or worsening of the situation. On the other hand, aggressive patterns may be screaming, yelling, threatening, blaming, punishing, belittling, or guilt-tripping the other person during an attempt at communication.

Barrier 2: Inability to Identify Needs

When we cannot identify our needs in a given situation, we lose the ability to be assertive because we don't know what we need to be assertive about. This happens when you become so overwhelmed by your emotions during the conflict that you can't remember how you got in the situation in the first place or what you originally wanted to achieve. It's important that you can clearly identify your needs during a conflict or conversation.

Barrier 3: Negative Predictions

You've probably been in a situation where you could only think about the worst-case scenario. You couldn't see the facts of the situation because your mind was too focused on what could go *wrong* that it couldn't see what could go *right*. When we assume negative or bad things are going to happen in our relationship with another person, we lose sight of what the facts are and focus only on our thoughts and emotions.

Barrier 4: Overwhelming Emotions

Suppose you have learned patterns of being emotional during conflicts or grew up in a home where conflicts became very heated and emotional. In that case, your reaction to a similar situation would also become emotionally overwhelming. You become so overwhelmed by your emotions that you either explode during the conflict or conversation, or withdraw completely.

Barrier 5: Toxic Relationships

In some situations, no matter how hard we try or how much effort we put into the relationship, the other person remains engaged in behaviors that are harmful to us. In these relationships, the other person refuses to listen to your needs and wants, belittles you, threatens you, or blames you for the current conflict. You cannot change their behavior, and being assertive will not produce effective results.

Do any of these barriers seem familiar to you? Can you think of a current situation in which one of these barriers is preventing you from communicating clearly? If you can identify a barrier, how will you mindfully go about removing this barrier to make the communication between you and that person more effective?

Interactive Element: Assertiveness Scripts

Assertiveness is when you express your opinions, emotions, needs, and wants clearly, honestly, and respectfully without disregarding the other person's needs. In order for you to be assertive, you need to be able to identify your priorities and needs: What is it that you need from this relationship? And which of these needs do you find most important? You need to know what you want from this relationship and how to ask for these things. And it would be best if you were open to discussing and negotiating these needs and wants with the other person because their needs and wants matter too.

Assertiveness scripts are templates that you can use to help you think clearly when communicating something. Assertiveness is the middle ground between being aggressive and being passive. Assertive scripts can help you understand what you want to communicate by identifying what needs to be asserted in the relationship.

Below are three assertiveness scripts you can use to express yourself:

- I think _______

- I feel _______

- I want _______

"I think" is about expressing the facts of the situation as well as your perception of the situation and these facts. Avoid attacking or judging the other person as you do this. Don't make assumptions about how they feel or what their opinions are. You don't know what they are thinking or feeling.

"I feel" is about expressing your emotions. It describes what you feel because of the other person's actions and behavior. Again do not attack, judge, or assume anything about the other person's emotions. Express only the emotions *you* are experiencing.

"I want" is about conveying the needs you were trying to communicate. This is a rather tricky one as you should keep several things in mind: don't ask the other person to change how they feel or think. Instead, ask for a behavioral change and be specific. Also, don't request several things. Focus on one thing that's doable for them.

Our interpersonal effectiveness skills are vital to our relationships and our mental, emotional, and physical health. We don't experience unnecessary anxieties and suffering when our relationships are good; instead, we have relationships in which we communicate effectively and work through problems rather than allowing them to fester and the pain to be prolonged. In the following chapter, we are going to help you learn three skills of interpersonal effectiveness that will help you become more effective in your communication and relationships with others.

Chapter 13: Skills and Techniques

Be honest, brutally honest. That is what's going to maintain relationships. —Lauryn Hill

Interpersonal effectiveness has three goals. As we mentioned, each of these goals focuses on helping you improve your relationships with others, maintaining healthy relationships, and ensuring you are respected in these relationships.

In this chapter, we are going to introduce a set of skills for each of these goals and guide you through the process of using these skills in your relationships with others and understanding how they will not only improve your relationships with others but improve your sense of self-worth, self-respect and your confidence in interacting with others and maintaining healthy boundaries to protect yourself mentally, emotionally and physically.

Objective Effectiveness: DEAR MAN

A healthy relationship is about learning to get along with others, but it's also about asserting your own needs in these relationships. Finding the balance between our needs and those of others can be difficult, even more so when we need to be assertive but not aggressive or neglectful of our own needs.

DEAR MAN is a set of skills that will help you learn how to communicate effectively and be assertive with your needs and wants. This set of skills helps you ask for what you need, say 'no' to a request, and express your feelings constructively. DEAR MAN can be used in various relationships, from those between you and your parents, your siblings, school peers, friends, teachers, and other people in your life. Suppose you struggle to communicate your needs and wants in your interpersonal relationships. In that case, DEAR MAN teaches you how to improve on your communication skills and build stronger relationships that are often difficult when struggling with anxiety, worry, or other negatively intense emotions that hinder communication.

Worksheet for Teens

DEAR MAN is an acronym. Each letter stands for a specific skill that you'll be using during interactions with others to be assertive in your needs and wants but also to bring balance to these relationships where there might be more give than take or more take than give.

Since you are new to this skill set, it's best to start off by writing down all the information for each one. Once you are confident enough in your abilities to exercise this skill set, you will be able to use DEAR MAN in any situation without needing to write down all the details.

Describe

Describe the situation objectively. To be objective means only to state the facts. It's not about stating your opinions, interpretations, perceptions, or thoughts about the situation. The goal of this step is to get everyone on the same page. This is done by speaking to the other person about what in this interaction/relationship you are reacting to. What has happened to bring you to a point where you need to be assertive and state your needs?

Express

Express your feelings, opinions, perceptions, and interpretations of the situation. But do not assume that the other person knows how you feel or is aware of how their actions have impacted you. Therefore, be clear that these are _your_ assertions by using 'I' statements.

You can use the following statement to express yourself: "I feel____when______" or "I feel____because____." By using 'I' statements, you are not judging or assuming how the other person is feeling or what they are thinking. Instead, you are expressing how _their_ actions or words have negatively affected _you_.

Assert

At this point, you are clearly going to express what you need or want. Be specific about your requests or instructions. The other person cannot read your mind, so be straightforward and assertive about what it is that you want or say 'no' clearly.

For example, if you need to study for a makeup test and your friends want to hang out, you need to be assertive in saying 'no' to their request and not saying "Well, maybe later" or "I'll let you know" because these statements aren't assertive. Instead, you are leaving room for your friends to step over the line and push you to agree and neglect your own needs.

Think about how you will tell them what you need. Does it sound assertive without being aggressive or submissive? Write down precisely what you want to say so that you are not tempted to say something else.

Reinforce

This step is about rewarding those who respect or respond well to your needs and reinforcing your needs when they aren't being respected. Start by explaining the positive effects of getting what you want or need. If necessary, explain the negative consequences. When the other person responds well to your assertiveness and request, reward them with a smile or by saying "thank you". Write down how you will reward them for responding well. Write down how you will clarify or reinforce the consequences and highlight the positive effects.

For example, if your friends respect your need to study, you will thank them either by saying the words or by smiling. But suppose they continue to push and ignore your request. In that case, you might inform them that a failing grade will cause you to be grounded, meaning you will be spending less time with them, or that if they cannot respect this need, then you aren't sure they have your best interests at heart. Reinforcing isn't always easy but is often needed.

Mindfulness

During this interaction, there is a specific outcome you are working towards. This step is about focusing on these goals and maintaining your position. Don't allow yourself to be sidetracked. If you have to sound like a broken record, then do it. Mindfulness is about understanding your goals and needs during this interaction but also about keeping your emotions from becoming overwhelmed by the situation or ignoring your feelings.

If the other person starts to attack, threaten, or change the subject to divert you from stating your needs or from saying a clear 'no', do not respond to these attempts. Just keep being mindful—using your Wise Mind as you've been taught—to state your needs clearly. You have practiced the necessary skills to remain cool-headed during this encounter...now use that skill!

Write down the possible ways that the other person can try to sidetrack you or attempt to divert the conversation. What topics might distract you from this goal? Write them down and remind yourself of the goal in the face of these distractions.

Appear Confident

It's important that when you communicate your needs, or when you are saying 'no', that your body, voice, and tone clearly say this as well. Be mindful of how you speak, your tone of voice, and your body language. Describe your posture and eye contact. Be specific. Be confident in what you are saying, even if you don't feel it.

For example, if you are going to stare at the floor and whisper your 'no', the other person might see this as a non-assertive need and overstep. When you appear vulnerable or unsure about what you are communicating, people will see this as an opening to push you to obey their wants and needs.

So, in the example with your friends, if you were whisper 'no' or laugh off their request to come hang with them, they will not realize that you are being serious and might think you just need convincing. Instead of understanding your needs, they will overstep these needs and hurt you—often without realizing. Therefore, stand tall, keep your voice calm but assertive, maintain eye contact with them, and clearly speak the words you want to say—ensuring you are being heard.

Negotiate

You aren't always going to get what you want, the same as the other person isn't always going to get what they want. Relationships require that you compromise from time to time. Be willing to negotiate. Be willing to give to get. Offer other solutions. Say 'no' but offer to do something else instead.

This step can be tricky but requires that you maintain your boundaries when negotiating. If your goal is to be given the time and space to study, do not compromise by spending time with your friends before studying. Still say 'no' but offer to spend time with them after you've finished the test. Another example can be your mother asking you to clean the garage and rake the leaves. If you're pressed for time on assignments, you can express to your mother that you can do one of the two right now but that the other will have to wait until you've finished the assignment. This allows your mother to understand you aren't refusing to do the chores in general but that your school work is taking priority. Perhaps she'll offer some other solution to this.

During this step, it is best to focus on what will work for both of you. This can often take time and might be frustrating, but once you both state your needs, you will be able to find a middle ground that will work.

Relationship Effectiveness: GIVE

Objective effectiveness is about stating your needs in a relationship. But relationships aren't all about getting what *you* want, but are about the other person too. The acronym GIVE represents a useful set of skills to help you improve and maintain the relationships you value by fostering positive interactions in these relationships.

Worksheet for Teens

GIVE can be used in any of the relationships you have with others. Practicing these skills regularly in your relationships will not only improve them but make them stronger as you become more aware of the importance of truly listening, validating, and being kind and gentle during interactions—especially those that are difficult.

Be <u>G</u>entle

Be gentle, kind, and respectful. Avoid attacking the other person, making threats, or using manipulation. Do not harass them or make threatening statements. Avoid body language or actions that appear judgmental, blaming, or demoralizing, such as smirking, rolling your eyes, or interrupting the other person.

Be respectful and graceful, and remain in the discussion even if it's uncomfortable or painful. Understand the possible reasons why the person is feeling the way they are, why they have these opinions or have made these decisions. Even if you don't agree with them, you can still be respectful. Be prepared to accept the occasional 'no'.

Act Interested

Truly listen to what the other person is conveying through their thoughts and feelings. See the situation from their perspective. When we interact with someone who appears interested, we respond well to the interaction and become open to opinions and thoughts. Therefore it's important that even if we do not want to be interested in the interaction, that we do all we can to appear interested. Keep eye contact, lean towards the person instead of away from them, and keep your body language open.

If you're asking yourself if acting interested is being dishonest, remember opposite action. The goal of opposite action is about doing what is most effective, and in this situation, what is most effective is that you appear interested even when you are not. *Acting* interested can also lead to you *becoming* interested.

Validate

Validate the other person's thoughts and feelings. This means expressing that you understand what the other person's opinions and perspectives are and expressing that you can sympathize with why they are feeling the way they are. As with radical acceptance, validating is not the same as agreeing. You can validate someone's thoughts and feelings without agreeing to their actions or decisions.

This skill is useful during disagreements because it allows you to understand the other person's actions better. Practicing validation regularly can make your relationship with that person stronger. It also allows you to understand the other people in your life better.

Use an <u>E</u>asy Manner

Difficult situations are hard enough as is. It does not mean the interaction needs to be as tense and painful. Instead, approach these interactions with a bit of humor, lightheartedness, and a smile. Even if you and this person disagree on something, the conversation doesn't have to be one in which you are standing opposed to each other. Use a light and easygoing tone to soothe these situations and leave your attitude at the door.

Is there any current relationship that you feel is worth maintaining and improving upon? How can you use the skills listed above to help you maintain and improve these relationships?

Self-Respect Effectiveness: FAST

When we are communicating something important, whether in a discussion or an argument, it's important that we maintain our self-respect, remain truthful, and get our needs met without sacrificing our values.

Self-respect goals focus on what makes you feel moral, capable, and effective, respects your values and beliefs, and makes you like yourself. The FAST acronym will help you achieve self-respect effectiveness by ensuring you maintain these goals in your relationships with others.

Worksheet for Teens

The four FAST skills will teach you how to act during an argument while staying objective and respectful of your own values and integrity.

Be **F**air

Be fair to yourself and the other person. Be fair when you describe the situation or state your goal for this interaction. Be fair in considering the other person's wants and needs. Avoid being judgmental. Stick to the facts.

Don't Over-**A**pologize

If an apology isn't warranted, don't apologize. Don't apologize because you were asserting yourself in having an opinion or disagreeing. Don't apologize for asking for what you need or feeling the way you feel. Overly apologizing gives the other person the impression that you are wrong. Apologizing when you don't believe it will reduce your sense of effectiveness over time and minimize your self-respect. Constantly apologizing will also get on others' nerves. Only apologize when you were wrong, made a mistake, or hurt someone. You are allowed to take up space with your existence, thoughts, feelings, and opinions.

Stick to Your Values

Asking for change isn't easy. It can be scary because we might fear that the other person will stop liking us. Thinking this way leads to the risk of being sucked into agreeing to something we don't want or don't believe in. It can also result in us compromising on our values when we don't want to. Make sure you stick to your truth, values, and beliefs. You NEVER have to compromise on your values to avoid conflict or to please someone. Sticking to your values will increase your sense of self-worth over time.

Be **T**ruthful

Stick to the truth without shaping it to fit your wants or needs. Don't stretch the truth. Don't lessen or sugarcoat the truth, either. Don't exaggerate or act helpless when you aren't. This creates a pattern of dishonesty and will start to chip away at your self-respect. It will also cause the other person to have difficulty believing in the truth. Be truthful even when it's scary.

With a focus on the four skills above, reflect on the following questions. Can you identify where you are being ineffective?

- Do any of the four skills listed above appeal to you as a skill you'd like to engage in more? Why?

- Are you often apologizing for how you feel or for expressing a need or opinion? How can you change this using the above skill?

- Are you defaulting on your values or self-respect skills because you feel scared? Why do you feel this way?

- Do you neglect one of these skills because it allows you to avoid confrontation? Does it make it easier or safer for you to neglect your self-respect? Why, what are the facts, and do they match the situation?

In this chapter, we've provided you with three sets of skills focused on helping you be more effective in your relationships and interactions with others. GIVE and FAST taught you how to effectively interact or behave during interactions, whereas DEAR MAN helped teach you how to get your objectives met during these interactions. Each of these skills can be used separately or they can all be used together. As you become more practiced in these skills, it will become easier for you to use them during any interaction and to stand your ground when needed.

Remember, not all relationships are worth keeping, but all relationships worth keeping require that you are able to healthily and effectively maintain and improve upon them. Using the above skill sets will help you maintain and improve the relationships you value and want to keep strong.

Conclusion

One of the most peaceful mindsets ever begins the moment you finally find the courage to let go of what you can't change. It is what it is. Accept it, learn from it and move on. It doesn't matter what you've done; what matters is what you choose to do from here. —
Marc & Angel Chernoff

We started this journey feeling overwhelmed, out of control, and suffering under our anxieties and worries about our past and future. But even though this is the end of our current DBT journey, it's only the beginning of your journey to conquer your anxieties and cope with anything life throws your way.

In **Core Mindfulness**, we learned the *what* skills that taught us to **observe**, **describe**, and **participate** in every situation. We also learned the *how* skills that taught us to be **non-judgmental** during situations, to do things **one-mindfully**, and to be **effective** in the things we do. These skills helped train our rational and emotional minds to find their overlap: our **Wise Mind**. Our Wise Mind allows us to be cool-headed during situations while also being mindful of our emotions and thoughts on the situation.

During **Distress Tolerance**, we learned the objective is to be able to tolerate distressing moments, and that distress tolerance is about **ACCEPT**ing the things we cannot change, **RESISTT**ing overwhelming emotions that want to take control, **TIPP**ing our body's chemistry to reduce overwhelming emotions, **self-soothing** to bring ourselves relief from painful or distressing situations, **grounding** ourselves in the present moment, and weighing the **pros and cons** of our actions in every situation.

From **Emotion Regulation**, we became aware of the possible myths we hold when it comes to our emotions, such as that our emotions make us illogical or irrational, that expressing our emotions is a sign of weakness, that our emotions cannot be controlled, that feeling strong emotions means we are out of control, that our emotions speak our truths, and that we are our emotions. We learned that our emotions are our reactions to situations and that, with the right skills, we are able to control these reactions and lessen the intensity of our emotions.

We learned how to STOP a situation from escalating due to our intense emotions, use our ABC PLEASE skills to practice self-care during difficult times or when life becomes too busy. We also learned that positive self-talk is powerful, and that taking small steps when making changes or learning a new skill is a recipe for success. Lastly, we learned that there will be times when we need to do the opposite of what our emotions are influencing us to do because doing the opposite action is more effective and allows us to be intentional in our decisions, choices, and actions in life.

Lastly, we focused on **Interpersonal Effectiveness** and how our emotions, thoughts, and behaviors can impact others, and how our relationships with others can impact our mental, emotional, and physical well-being. **Objective effectiveness, relationship effectiveness,** and **self-respect effectiveness** are the three goals of interpersonal effectiveness. Each represents a specific objective during our interactions with others: objective effectiveness is about getting what we want; relationship effectiveness is about maintaining and improving relationships; and self-respect effectiveness is all about respecting ourselves during interactions so as to maintain our values and beliefs.

We learned that **DEAR MAN** could help us clearly and assertively state our needs in relationships. We learned that there is a **GIVE** and take in any relationship and that there will be times when we need to be stead**FAST** in our beliefs, values, needs, and interactions with others, but that it's also important we understand and validate the other person, that we see things from their point of view too. We also learned that maintaining and improving relationships takes courage, confidence, and standing our ground while being fair, gentle, and respectful of the other person. Lastly, we learned the importance of negotiating and compromising when it is effective to do so.

Now that you've worked through all four DBT modules and their related skills, you have the chance to decide how your life will be from this point on. You can't change the past, but you can change the present moment and make the future seem a lot brighter than it is right now. What happens from this point on is your choice. An **intentional** choice. You are the one in control of how you react to every emotion, thought, situation, and interaction.

The only difference between the previous times you wanted to take control of your anxieties and worries in life compared to now is that this time you have the skills you need to survive difficult moments and conquer your anxieties. This time you have an armory of skills at your disposal to help you through and make you more resilient and accepting of what has been.

Remember that even if you don't believe it yet, repeating and pretending that it's true will make it your truth. Therefore believe. Believe in everything inside you. Believe that you will survive. You will be stronger. You will heal. You will conquer your anxieties. Believe until it becomes your truth.

Most of all, remember that DBT skills need mastering. You need to practice these skills over and over again before you'll be able to use them more effectively in your daily life. These skills won't just be helpful for right now, but they'll be helpful for later in life too. Practice these skills as many times as you need or want until you're able to use them skillfully. Be kind to yourself. These skills take hard work, dedication, and patience to learn, but they will be so worth it!

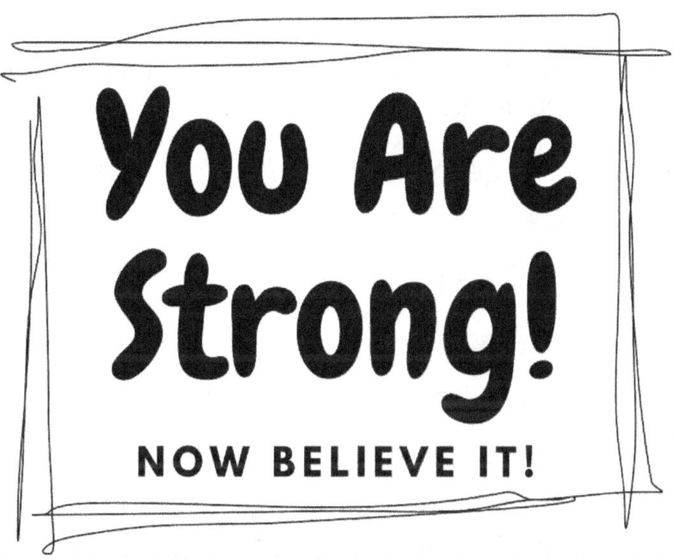

If you found this workbook helpful in calming down your thoughts, taking control of overwhelming situations, focusing on the present moment, and being effective in any situation or interaction, please leave a review. A review can help someone else struggling with anxiety, overwhelming and intense emotions, unhealthy relationships, and distressing situations learn how to cope, take control, and conquer their anxieties.

Please *leave us a review* for **The Anxiety Conquering Workbook for Teens?**

Are you ready to embark on a journey of conquering anxiety like never before? Well, if you've got your hands on **"The Anxiety Conquering Workbook for Teens,"** then you're in for a treat! But wait, before we dive into the details, let's talk about something amazing you can do to help others while relishing in your own fulfillment.

Have you ever stumbled upon a hidden gem, like a fantastic book, and wanted to shout about it from the rooftops? We've all been there, right? Now, imagine how fantastic it would feel to **help other teens** to experience the same benefits you did. That's where you come in!

Leaving a review for "The Anxiety Conquering Workbook for Teens" can do wonders for fellow readers. Not only will it guide them towards a life-changing resource, but it'll also make a real difference in their lives. Sharing your experience and thoughts through a review is like throwing a lifeline to someone who might be struggling with anxiety. You never know how your words might brighten their day and give them hope?

How do you leave a review? Just head over to Amazon and search **"The Anxiety Conquering Workbook for Teens"**, scroll down the page until you see the reviews section <u>bottom left</u> and click "write a customer review" or:

1. Go to the product detail page for the item. *If you've placed an order for the item, you can also go to* Your Orders

2. Click **Write a customer review.**

3. Click **Submit**.

Here is a video of step by step leaving a review on Amazon:
https://youtu.be/eyXrmVZv21w

The impact of **your review** can be tremendous. Think about the teens out there feeling lost and overwhelmed, searching for something that could **help them cope with anxiety**. Your review might be the beacon they need to find the support they've been craving. You could be the reason someone takes that first step towards a happier, more fulfilling life.

So, what are you waiting for? **Grab that keyboard or tap your way to the review section** and let your thoughts flow!

Thank you for being part of this journey, and remember, your words can change lives!

References

Ayeni, M. D. (2023, March 29). *25 dialectical behavioral therapy activities to raise emotionally intelligent kids.* Teaching Expertise. https://www.teachingexpertise.com/classroom-ideas/dbt-activity/

Bealing, J. (2014, September 25). *Brain scans reveal "grey matter" differences in media multitaskers.* The University of Sussex. https://www.sussex.ac.uk/broadcast/read/26540

Brach, T. (2003). *Radical acceptance: Embracing your life with the heart of a Buddha.* Bantam Dell.

Bradberry, T. (2014, October 8). *Multitasking damages your brain and career, new studies suggest.* Forbes. https://www.forbes.com/sites/travisbradberry/2014/10/08/multitasking-damages-your-brain-and-career-new-studies-suggest/?sh=5f667ce856ee

Bruce Lee Quotes. (n.d.). Goodreads. https://www.goodreads.com/quotes/3351420-emotion-can-be-the-enemy-if-you-give-into-your

CAMH. (2023). *Dialectical behavioural therapy.* The Center for Addiction and Mental Health. https://www.camh.ca/en/health-info/mental-illness-and-addiction-index/dialectical-behaviour-therapy

Chernoff, M. (2016, April 18). *10 quotes for turning an ending into a new beginning.* Marc and Angel Hack Life. https://www.marcandangel.com/2016/04/17/10-quotes-for-turning-an-ending-into-a-new-beginning/

Dos Santos, J. (2008, July 14). *Avatar: The Last Airbender* (No. S3E16) [TV Series Episode]. Nickelodeon Animation studio.

Gordon, S. (2021, July 26). *Everything your teen needs to know about setting boundaries.* Verywell Family. https://www.verywellfamily.com/boundaries-what-every-teen-needs-to-know-5119428

Ipsos MORI. (2019). *Perceptions of masculinity and the challenges of opening up.* Movember. https://cdn.movember.com/uploads/images/2012/News/UK%20IRE%20ZA/Movem ber%20Masculinity%20%26%20Opening%20Up%20Report%2008.10.19%20FIN AL.pdf

Klein, Y. (2020, February 4). *This one DBT skill can lift most teens' negative moods.* Evolve Treatment Centers. https://evolvetreatment.com/blog/dbt-skill-teens-moods/

Linehan, M. (2014). *DBT skills training manual* (2nd ed., pp. 170, 420). The Guilford Press.

Radical acceptance – DBT: Dialectical behavior therapy (2018). Dialectical Behavioral Therapy. https://dialecticalbehaviortherapy.com/distress-tolerance/radical-acceptance/

Razzetti, G. (2019, August 12). *Life is what happens when you are not on autopilot.* Personal Growth. https://medium.com/personal-growth/how-to-get-your-life-off-of-autopilot-4271defe9f61#:~:text=When%20we%20live%20on%20autopilot

Uitti, J. (2023, June 14). *The 20 best Lauryn Hill quotes.* American Songwriter. https://americansongwriter.com/the-20-best-lauryn-hill-quotes/

Watson, J. M., & Strayer, D. L. (2010). "Supertaskers: Profiles in extraordinary multitasking ability". *Psychonomic Bulletin & Review, 17*(4), 479–485. https://doi.org/10.3758/PBR.17.4.479

Image References

Agatha. (2022). Park City Park People [Image]. In *Pixabay.* https://pixabay.com/vectors/park-city-park-people-walk-stroll-7153125/

Altmann, G. (2017). Arrow Signpost Waypoint [Image]. In *Pixabay.* https://pixabay.com/illustrations/arrow-signpost-waypoint-direction-2085195/

GDJ, & Johnson, G. (2022). Mindfulness Brain Heart [Image]. In *Pixabay.* https://pixabay.com/vectors/mindfulness-brain-heart-mind-body-6911306/

GraphicMama-Team. (2016a). Detective Searching Man [Image]. In *Pixabay*. https://pixabay.com/vectors/detective-searching-man-search-1424831/

GraphicMama-Team. (2016b). Loudspeaker Man Boy [Image]. In *Pixabay*. https://pixabay.com/vectors/loudspeaker-man-boy-holding-1459128/

OpenClipArt-Vectors. (2013). Traffic Sign Stop [Image]. In *Pixabay*. https://pixabay.com/vectors/traffic-sign-stop-road-sign-157617/

Ordonez, A. (2017). River Cleansed Trees [Image]. In *Pixabay*. https://pixabay.com/vectors/river-cleansed-trees-nature-day-2831232/

Patel, B. (2019). Friends People Friendship [Image]. In *Pixabay*. https://pixabay.com/vectors/friends-people-friendship-family-4187953/

R, J. (2017). Battle Comic Fun [Image]. In *Pixabay*. https://pixabay.com/vectors/battle-comic-fun-election-campaign-2936446/

Saydaung, P. (2020). Children Faces Expressions [Image]. In *Pixabay*. https://pixabay.com/vectors/children-faces-expressions-emotions-5672087/

Steger, M. (2021). Pixel Cells Work Media Production [Image]. In *Pixabay*. https://pixabay.com/vectors/pixel-cells-work-media-production-6230152/